HAL LEONARD FINGERSTYLE GUITAR SONGS
GUITAR METHOD

PAGE

To access audio visit:
www.halleonard.com/mylibrary

5478-7381-4564-4587

ISBN 978-1-4584-2369-6

HAL•LEONARD®
CORPORATION
7777 W. BLUEMOUND RD. P.O. BOX 13819 MILWAUKEE, WI 53213

Visit Hal Leonard Online at
www.halleonard.com

Babe, I'm Gonna Leave You

Words and Music by Anne Bredon, Jimmy Page and Robert Plant

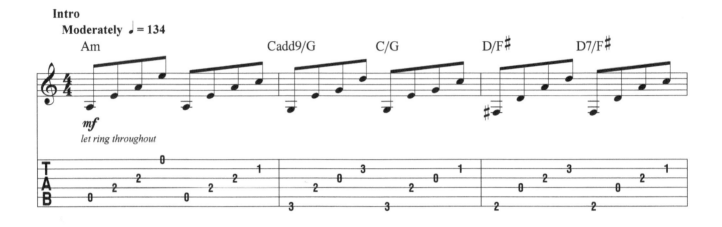

ba - by, ba - by, I'm ___ gon - na leave ___ you. ___

I said ___ ba - by, ___

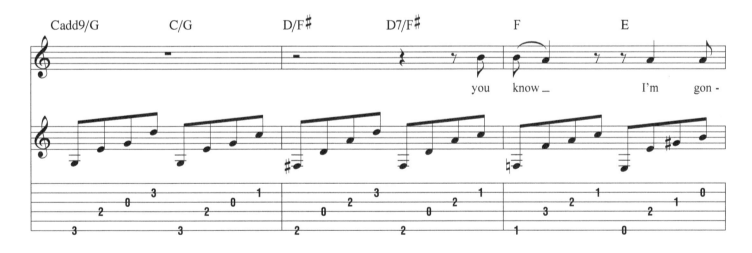

you know ___ I'm gon -

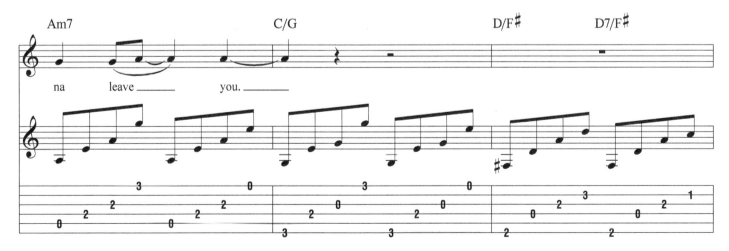

na leave ___ you. ___

3

I'll _____ leave you __ when __ the sum - mer - time, _____

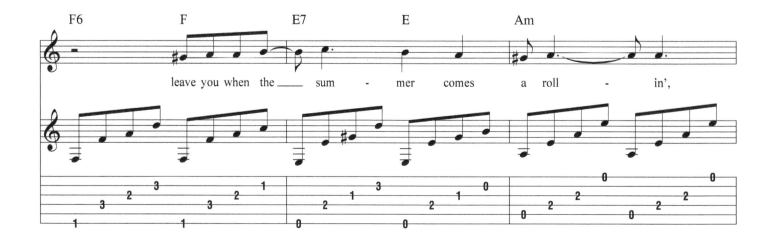

leave you when the ___ sum - mer comes a roll - in',

leave __ you when __ the sum - mer __ comes __

Interlude

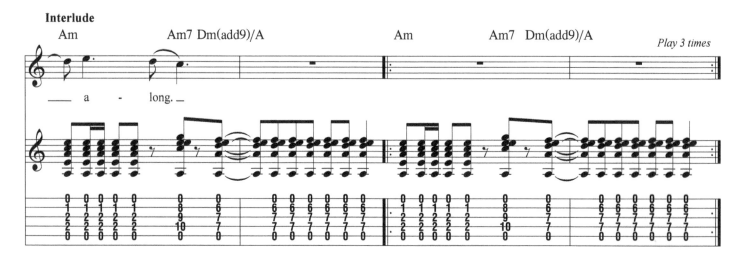

__ a - long. __

4

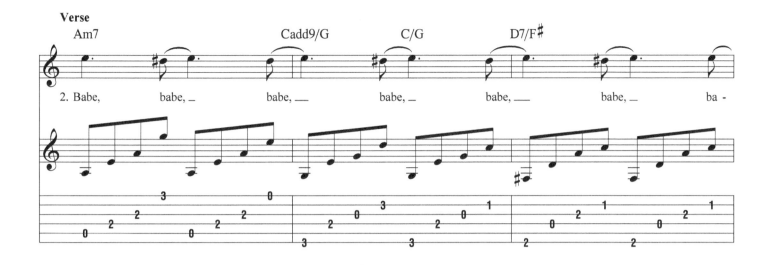

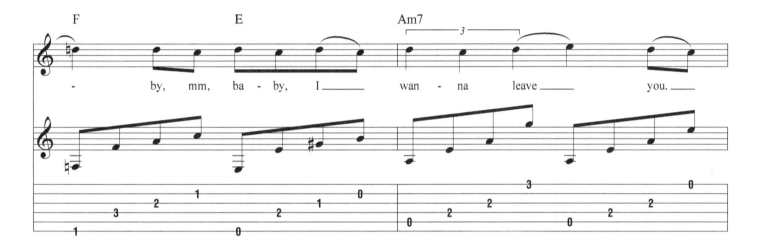

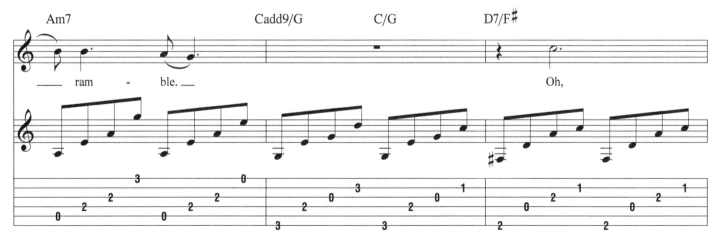

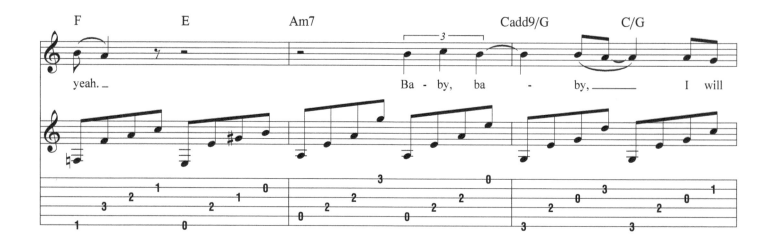

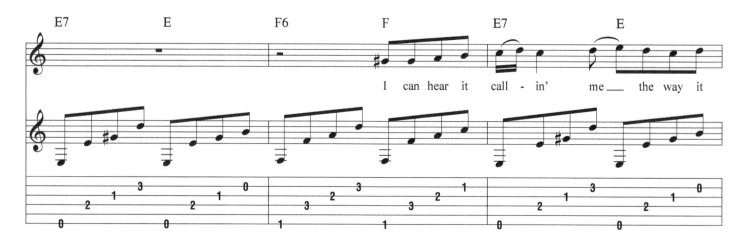

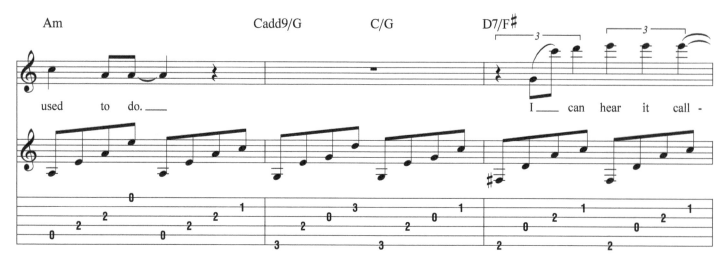

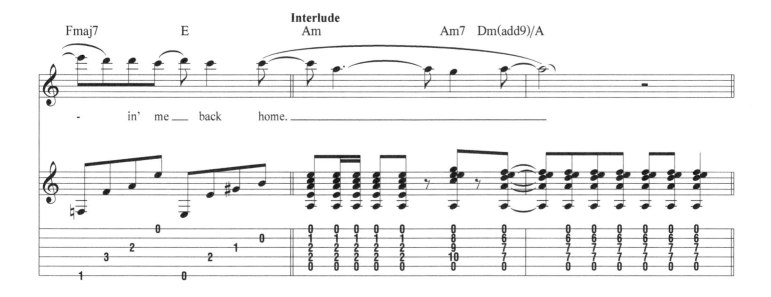

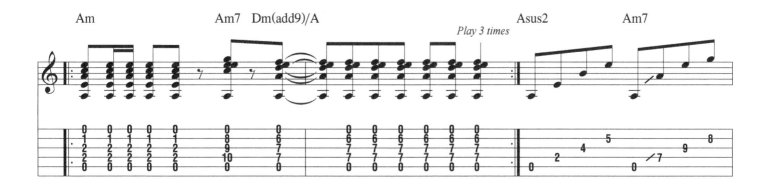

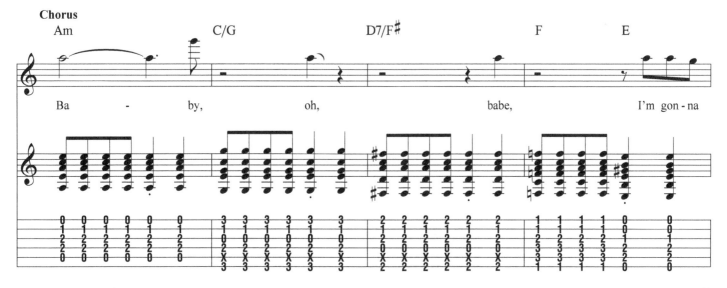

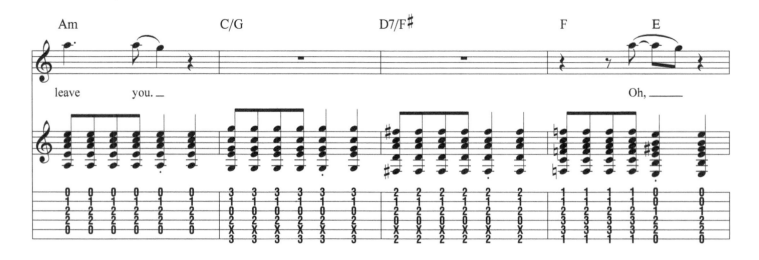

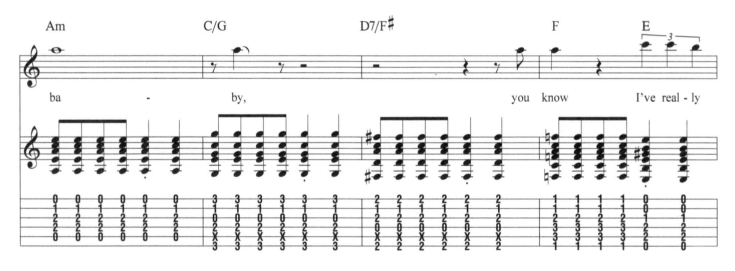

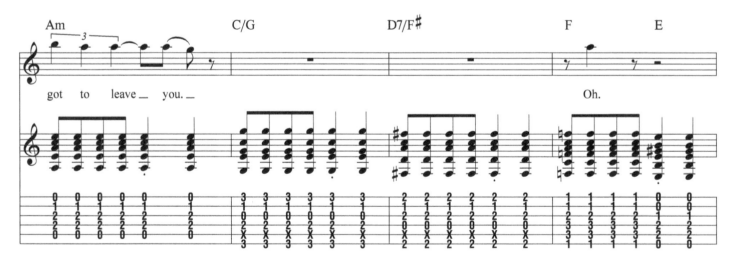

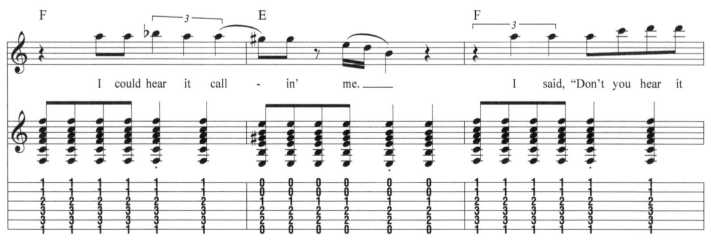

Interlude

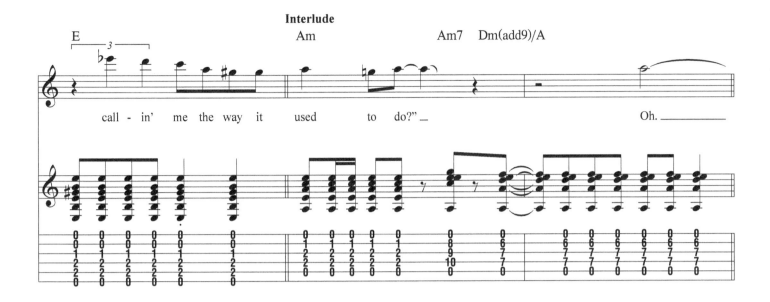

call - in' me the way it used to do?" __ Oh. _____

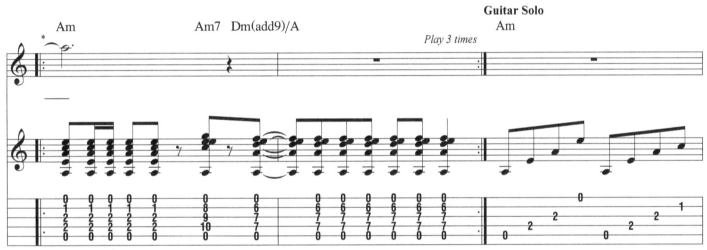

*Sing 1st time only.

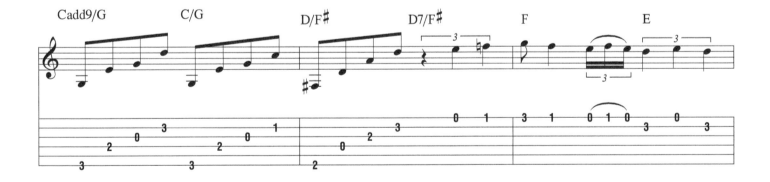

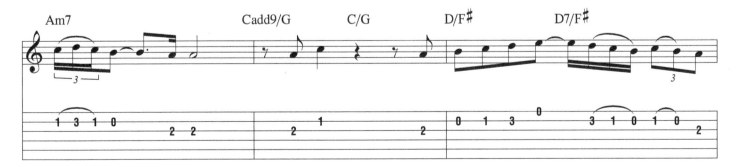

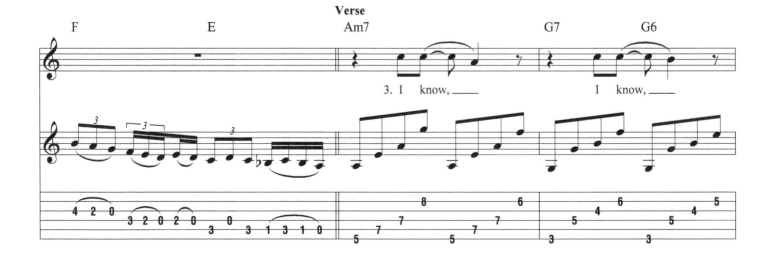

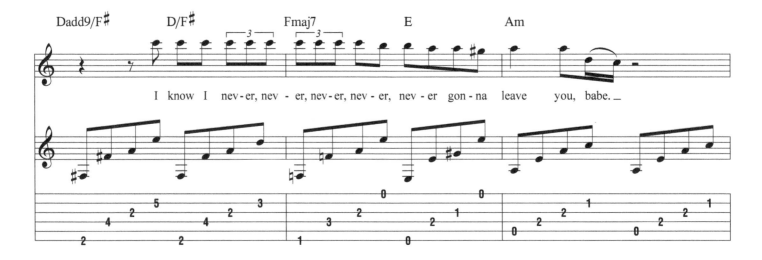

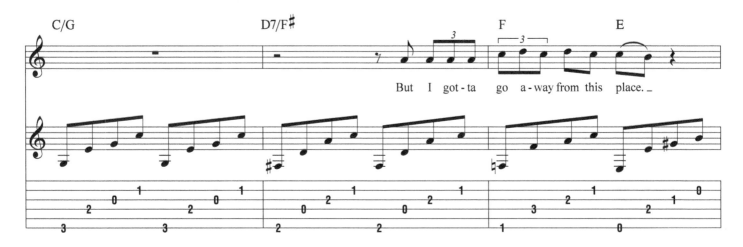

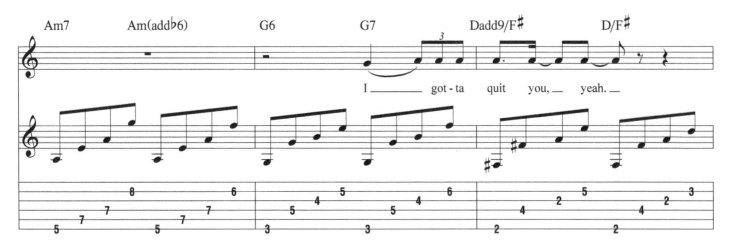

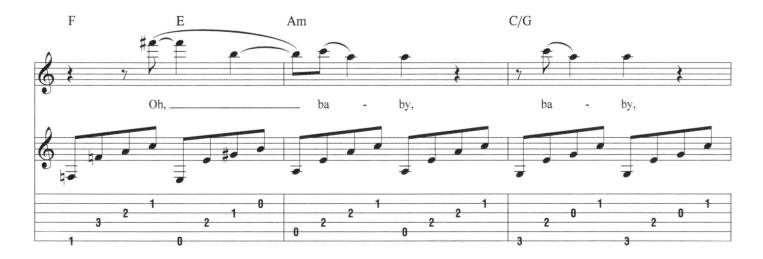

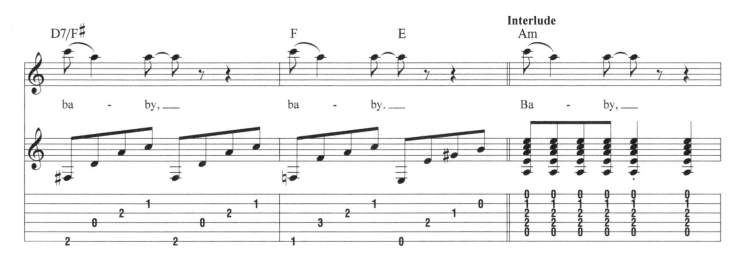

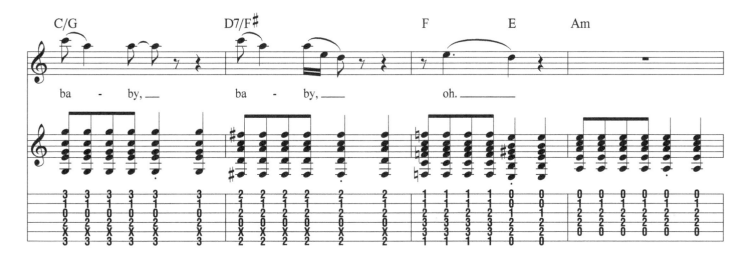

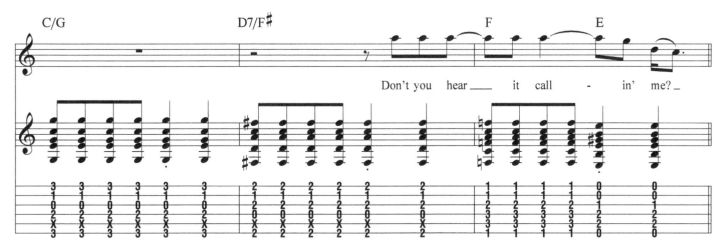

Verse

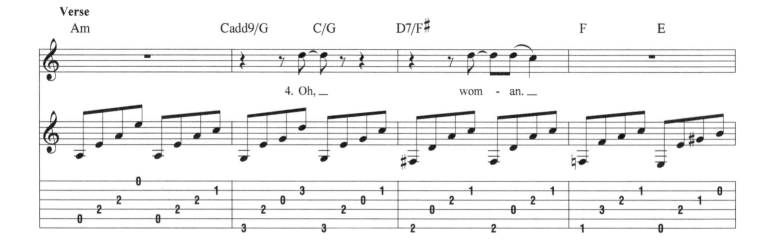

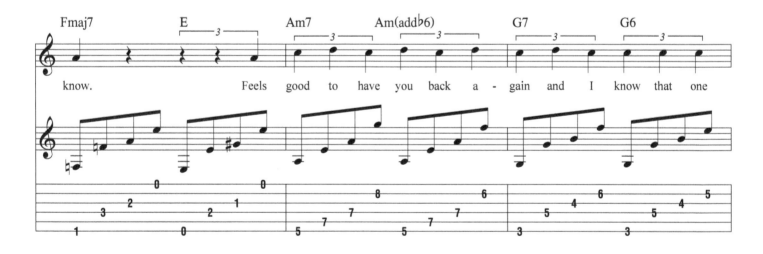

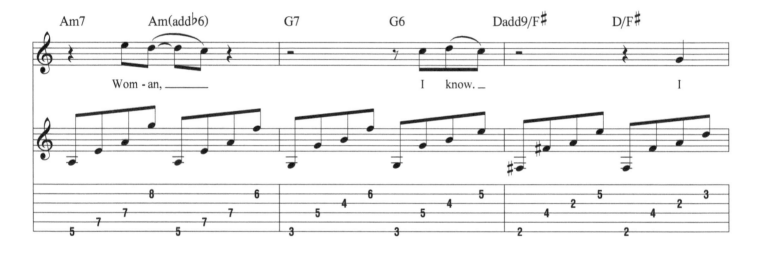

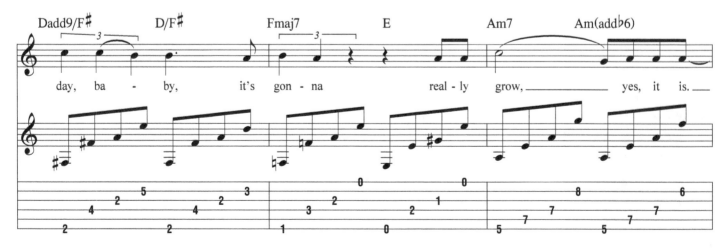

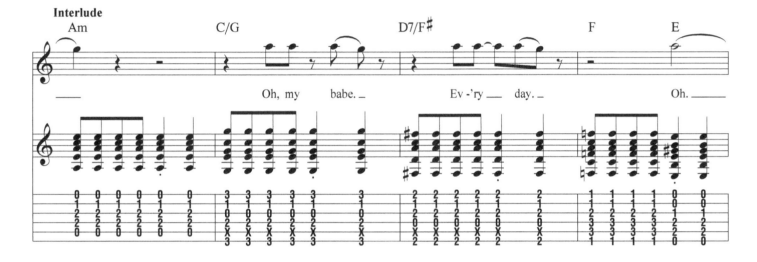

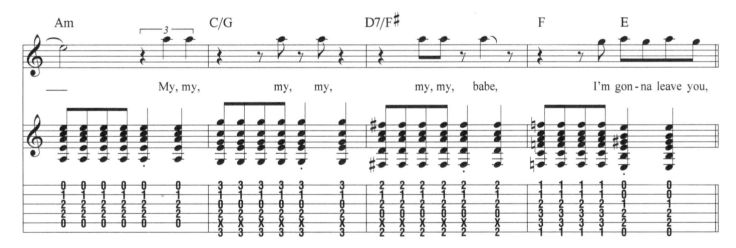

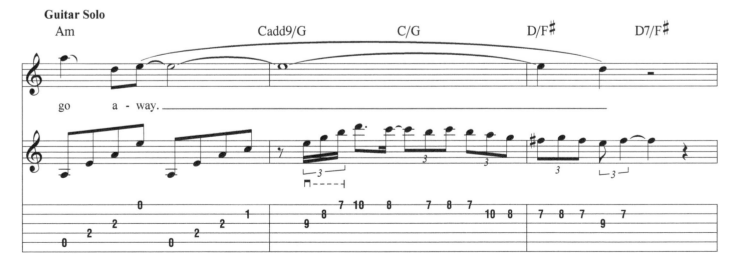

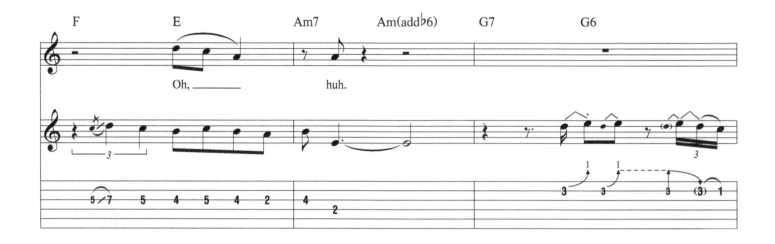

Oh, _____ huh.

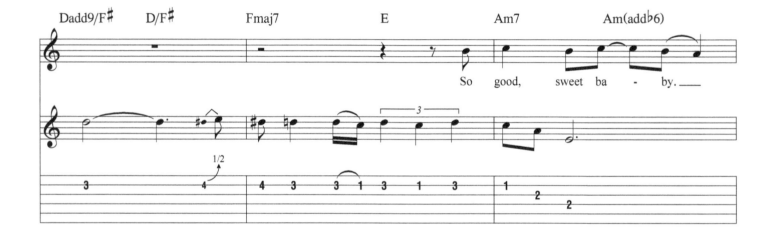

So good, sweet ba - by. ___

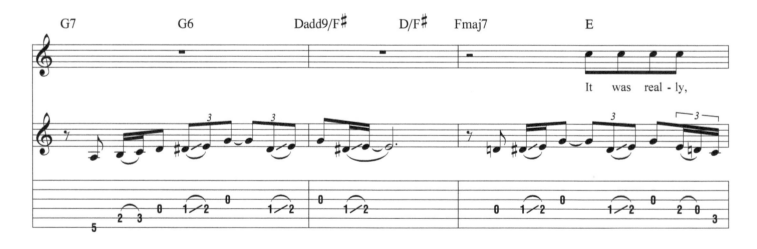

It was real - ly,

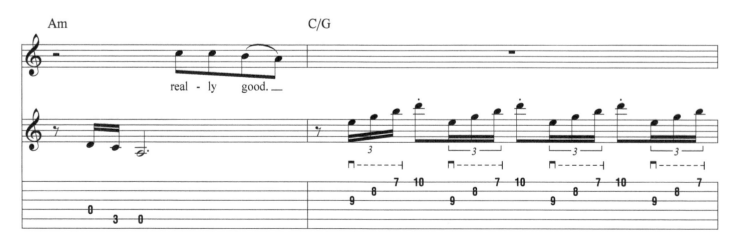

real - ly good. ___

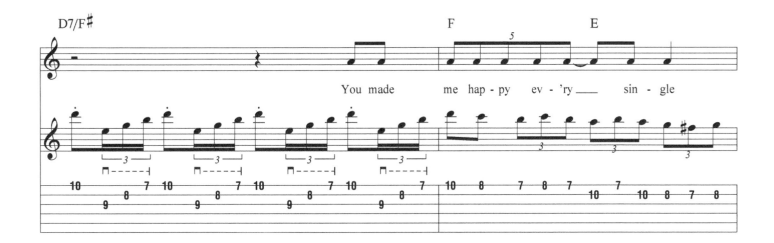

You made me hap-py ev-'ry_____ sin-gle

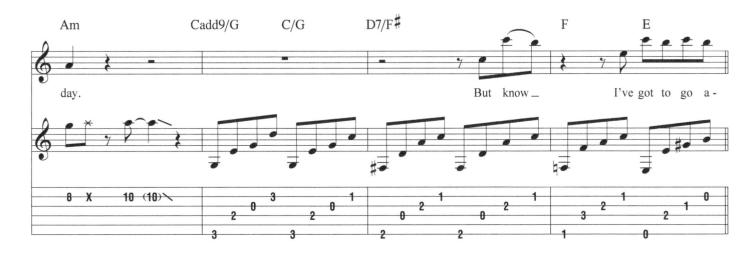

day.   But know___   I've got to go a-

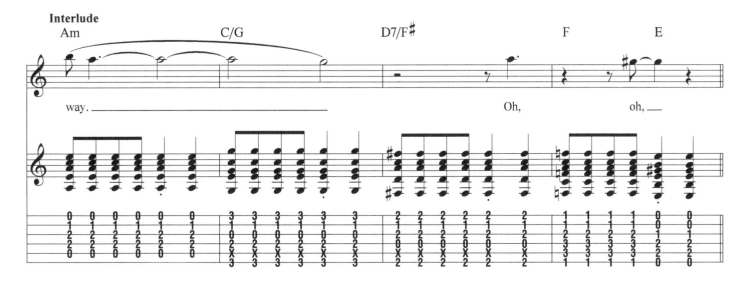

Interlude

way. _____   Oh,   oh,___

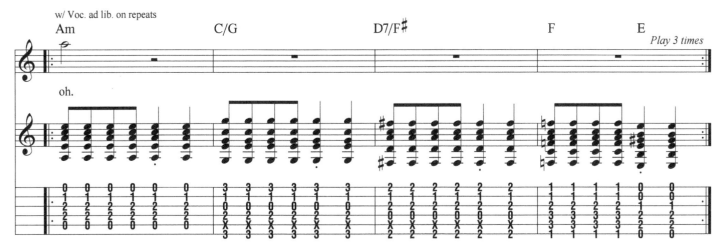

w/ Voc. ad lib. on repeats

Play 3 times

oh.

Outro
Free time

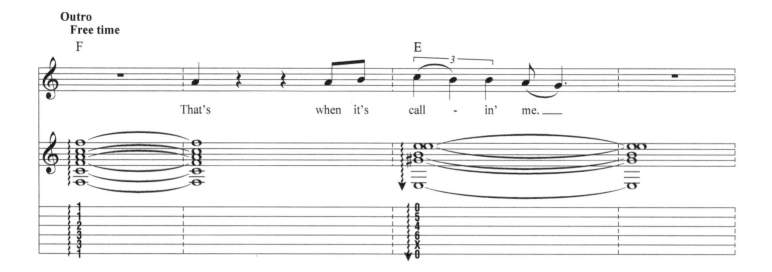

That's when it's call - in' me. ___

I said, "That's when it's call - in' me _____

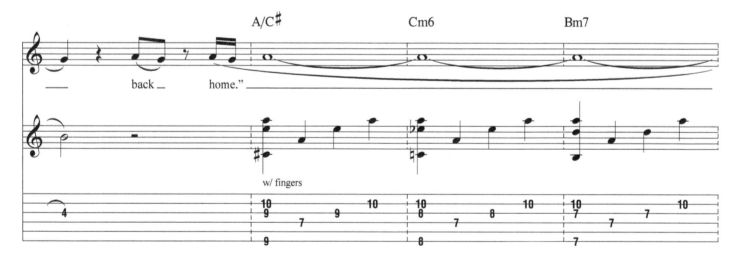

___ back __ home." _____

w/ fingers

Blackbird

Words and Music by John Lennon and Paul McCartney

*Strum upstemmed notes w/ index finger of pick hand
whenever more than one upstemmed note appears.

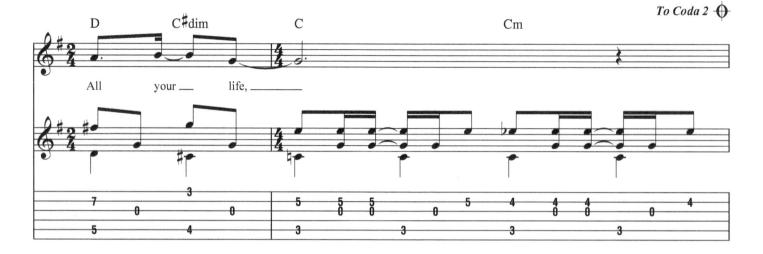

All your ___ life, _____

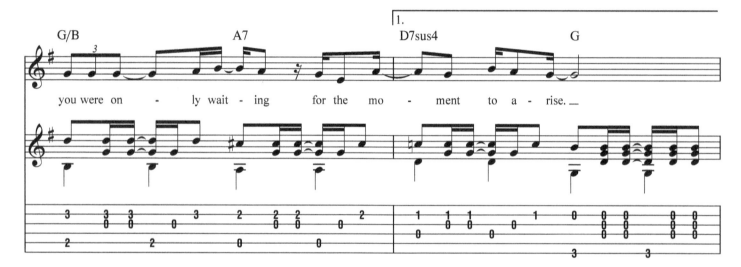

1.

you were on - ly wait - ing for the mo - ment to a - rise. ___

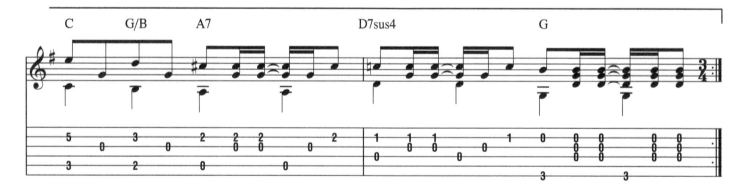

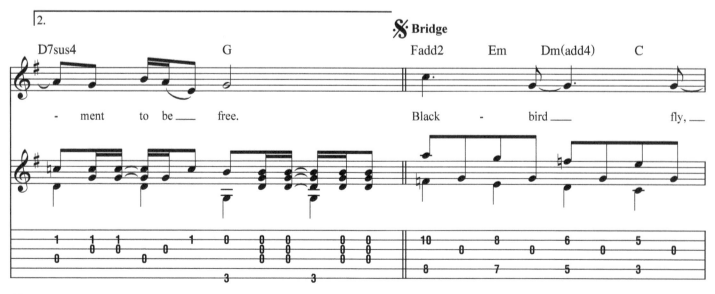

- ment to be ___ free.   Black - bird ___   fly, ___

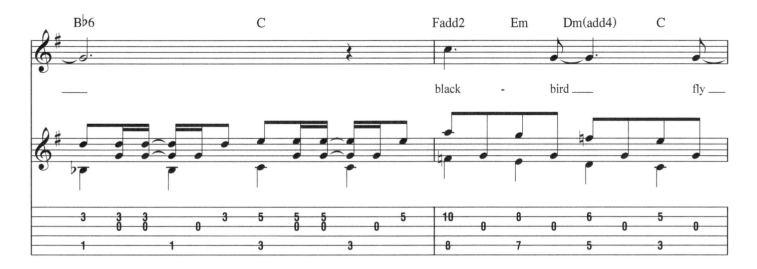

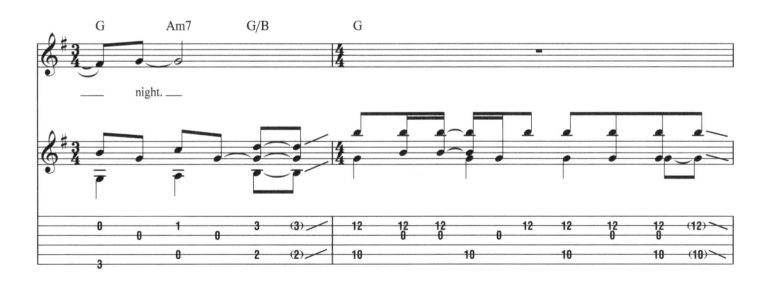

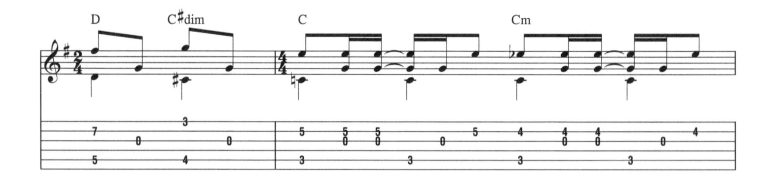

D.S. al Coda 1

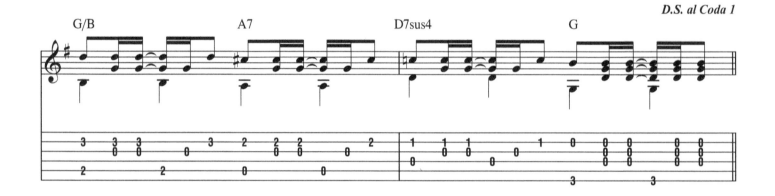

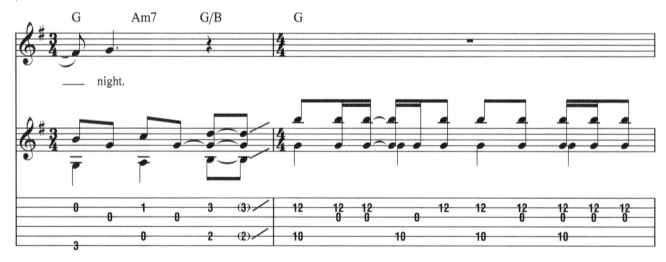

⊕ Coda 1

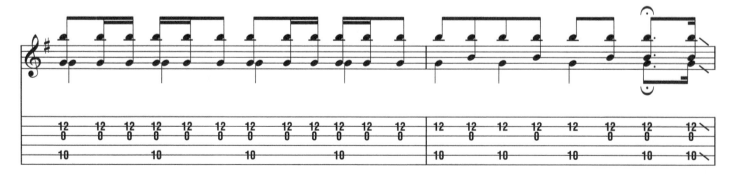

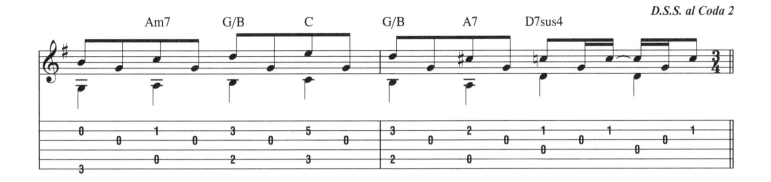

⊕ Coda 2

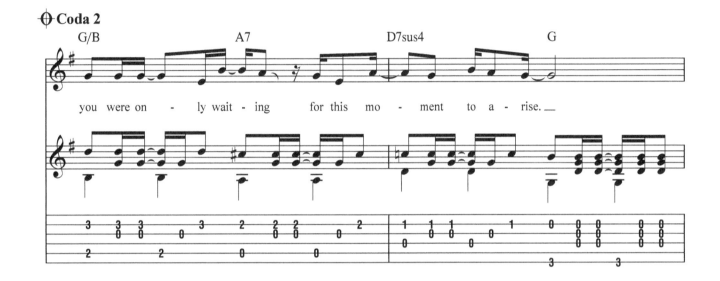

you were on - ly wait - ing   for this mo - ment to a - rise. __

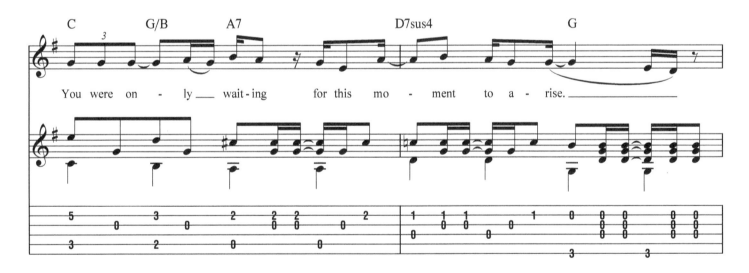

You were on - ly __ wait - ing   for this mo - ment to a - rise. _____

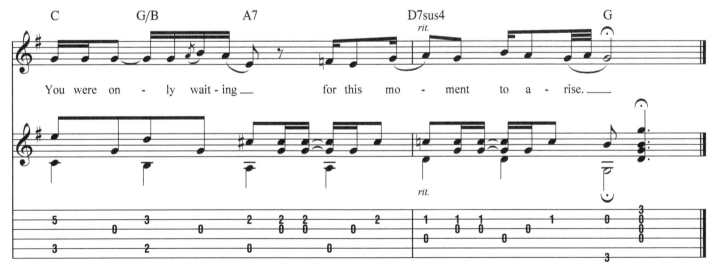

You were on - ly wait - ing __   for this mo - ment to a - rise. __

Classical Gas

Music by Mason Williams

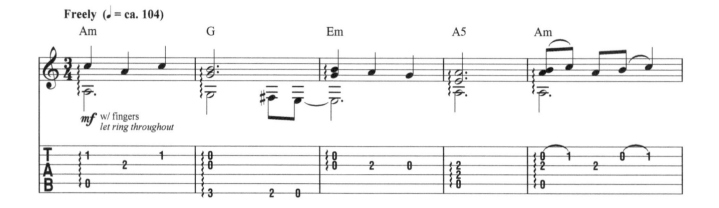

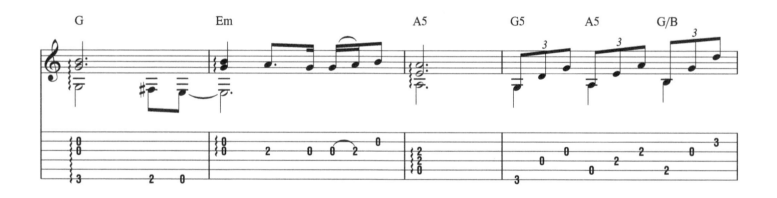

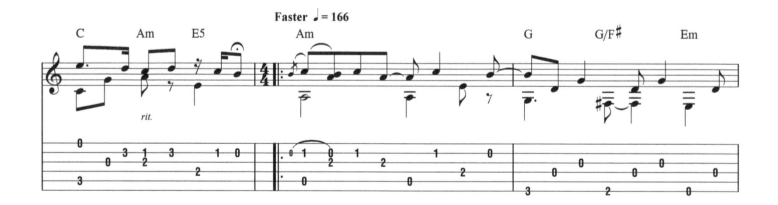

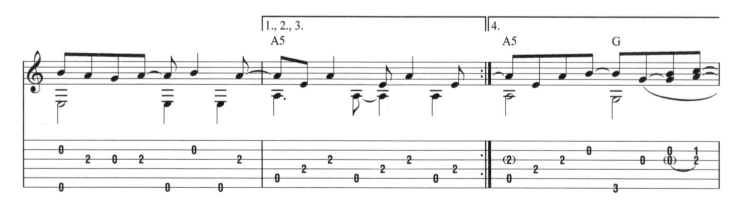

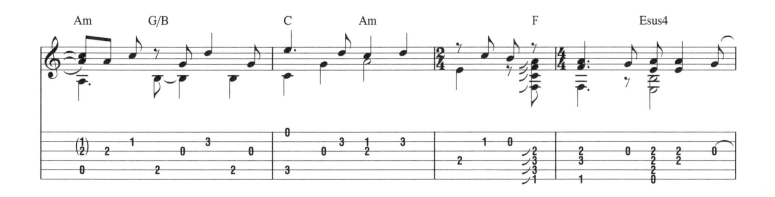

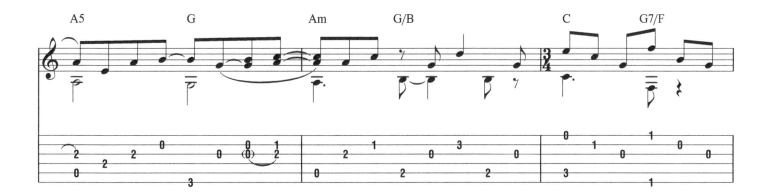

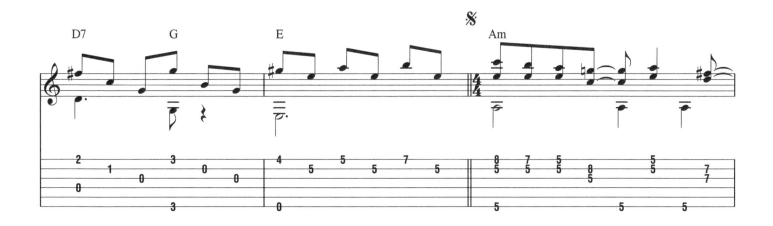

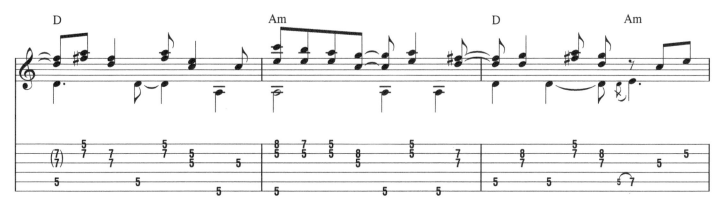

D　　　　　　G　　　　C/G　　　F　　　Bb/F

To Coda ⊕

Asus4

Dm(add9)/A

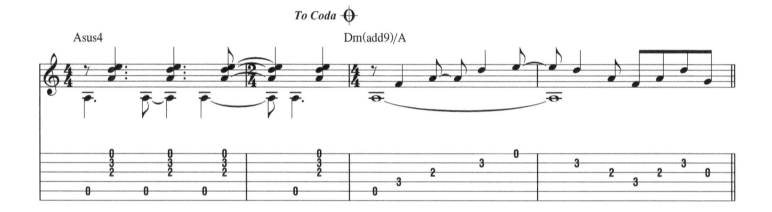

Am

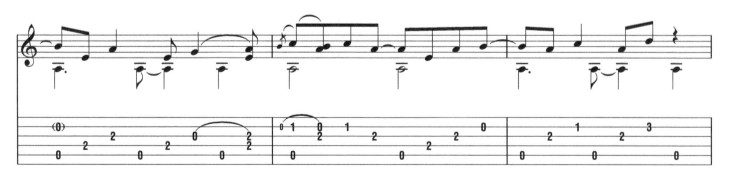

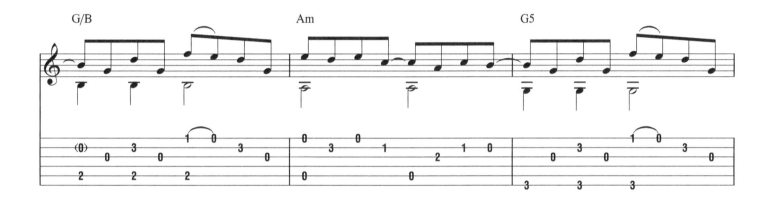

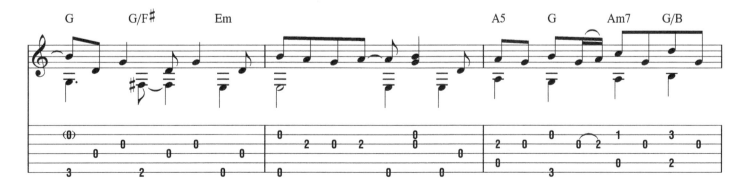

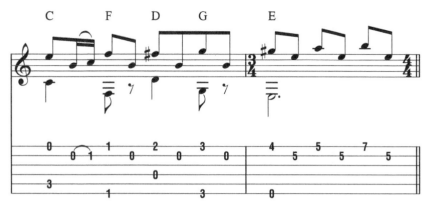

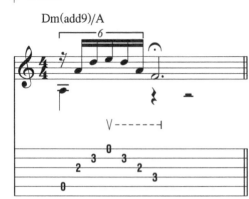

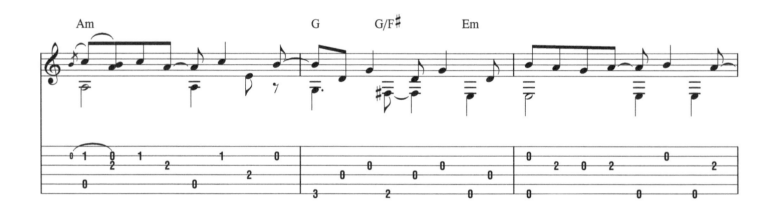

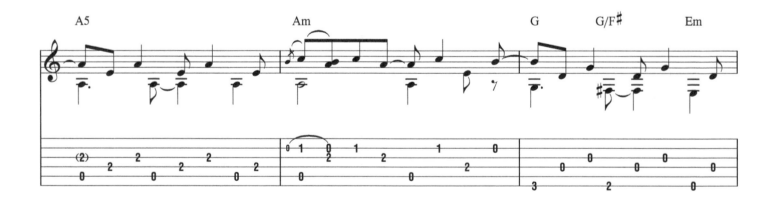

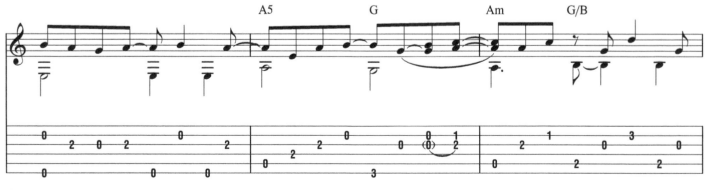

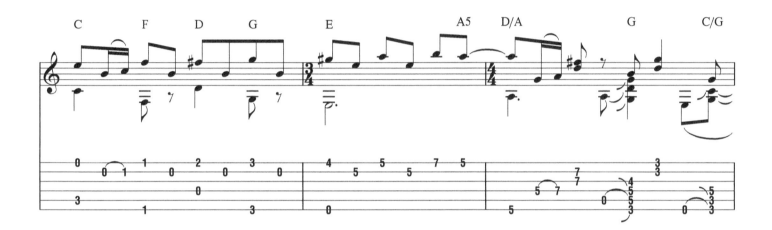

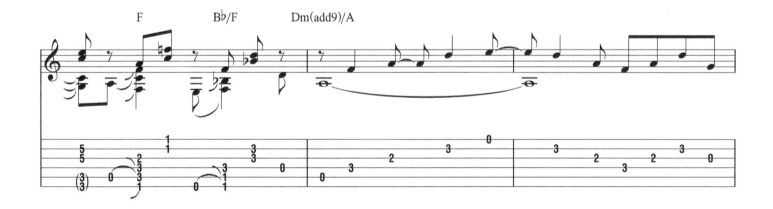

Don't Think Twice, It's All Right

Words and Music by Bob Dylan

Capo IV

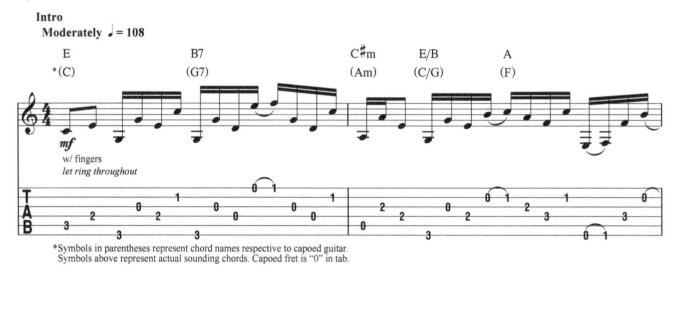

*Symbols in parentheses represent chord names respective to capoed guitar.
Symbols above represent actual sounding chords. Capoed fret is "0" in tab.

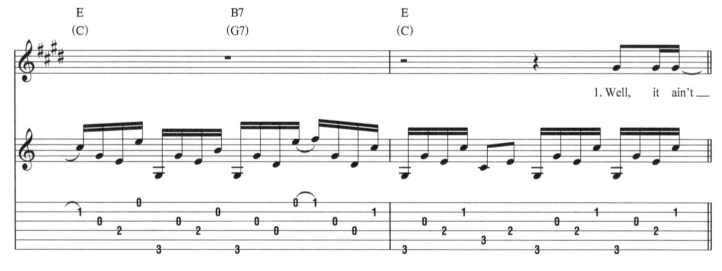

1. Well, it ain't

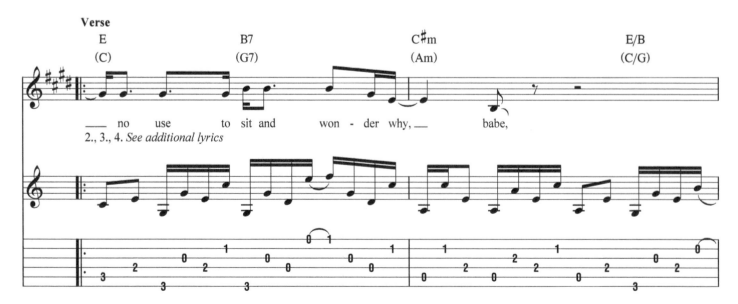

_ no use to sit and won-der why, _ babe,
2., 3., 4. *See additional lyrics*

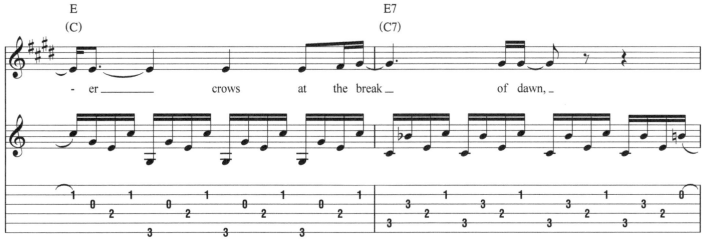

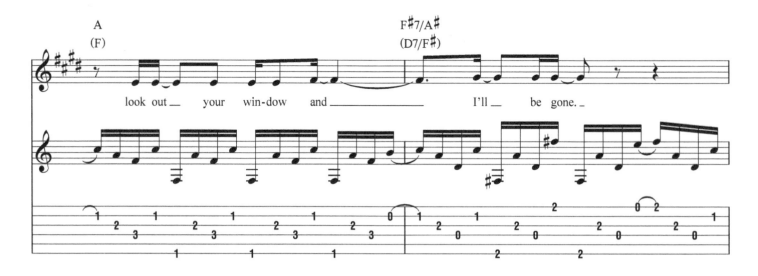

look out ___ your win-dow and ___ I'll ___ be gone. ___

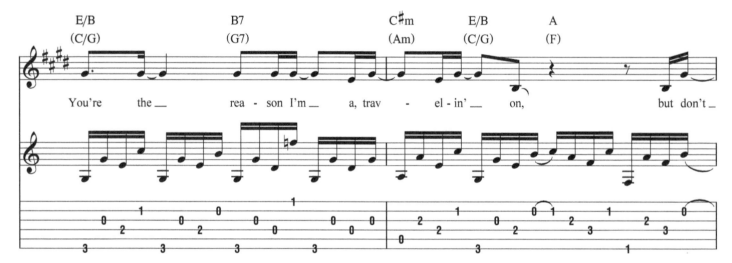

You're the ___ rea - son I'm ___ a, trav - el - in' ___ on, but don't ___

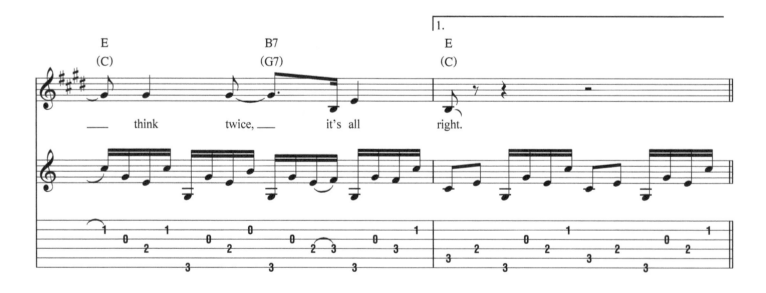

think twice, ___ it's all right.

Interlude

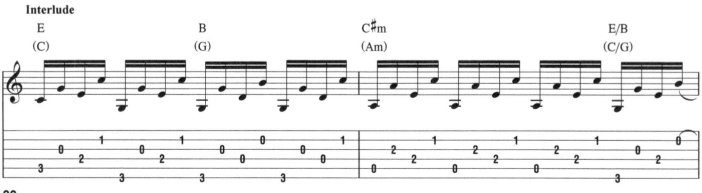

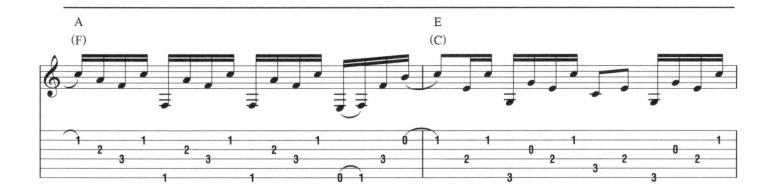

A
(F)

E
(C)

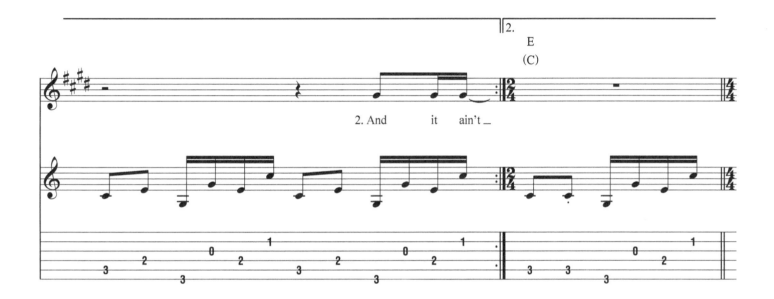

2.
E
(C)

2. And   it   ain't _

Interlude

E
(C)

B7
(G7)

C#m
(Am)

E/B
(C/G)

A
(F)

E
(C)

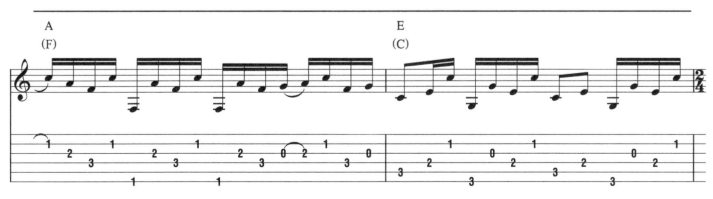

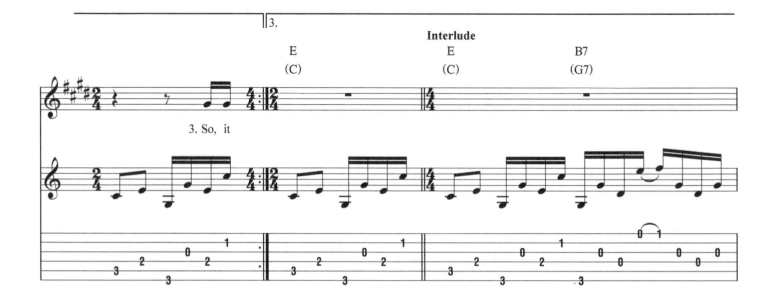

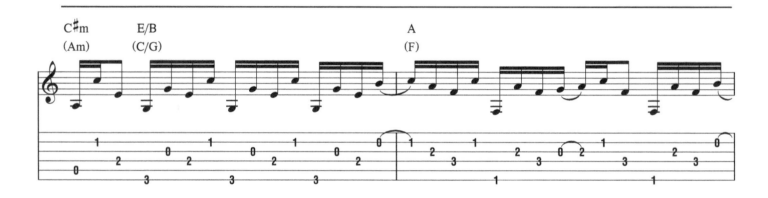

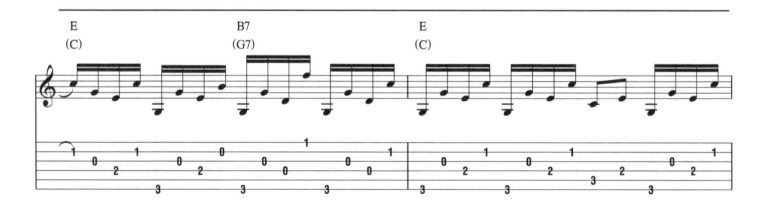

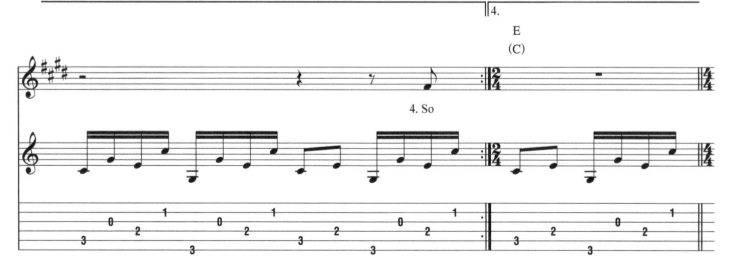

Outro

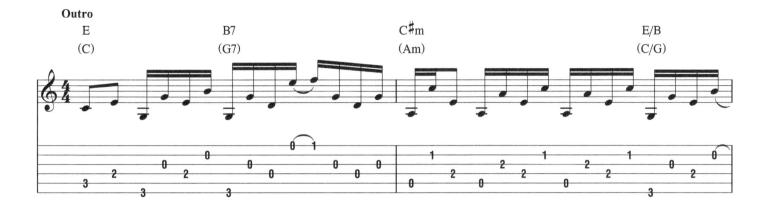

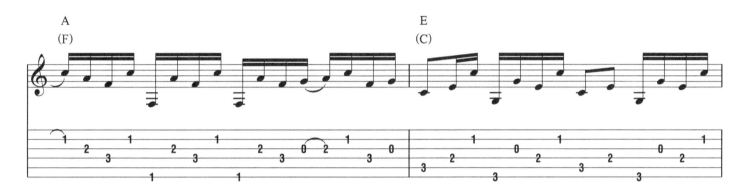

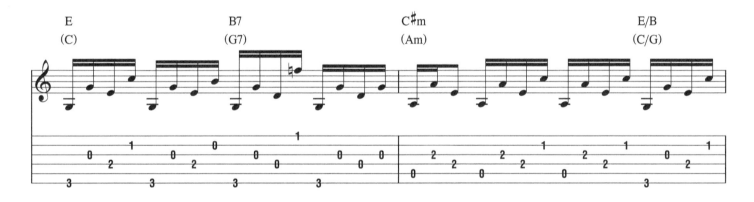

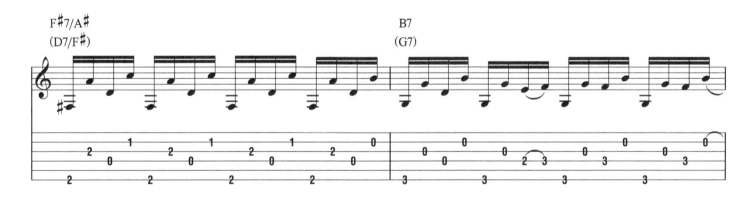

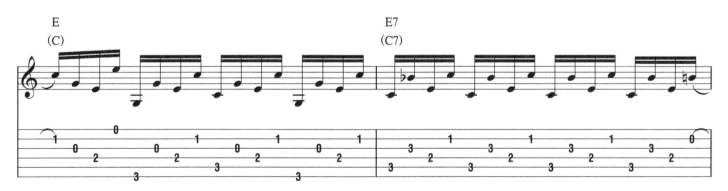

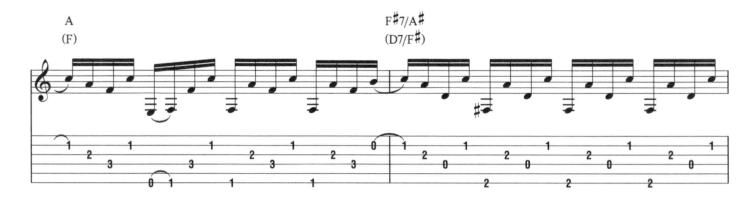

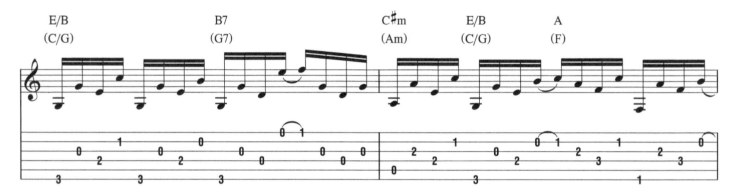

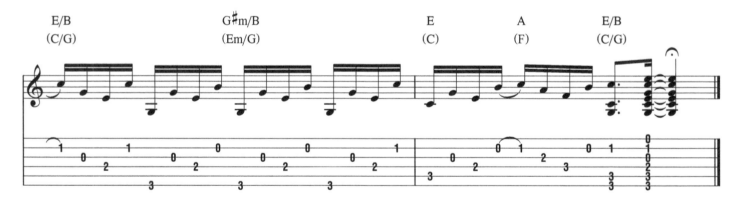

Additional Lyrics

2. And it ain't no use in turnin' on your light, babe,
   The light I never knowed.
   And it ain't no use in turnin' on your light, babe.
   I'm on the dark side of the road.
   But I wish there was somethin' you would do or say
   To try and make me change my mind and stay.
   But we never did too much talkin' anyway,
   But don't think twice, it's all right.

3. So it ain't no use in callin' out my name, gal,
   Like you never done before.
   And it ain't no use in callin' out my name, gal.
   I can't hear you anymore.
   I'm a, thinkin' and a, wonderin', walkin' down the road.
   I once loved a woman, a child I am told.
   I give her my heart but she wanted my soul,
   But don't think twice, it's all right.

4. So long, honey, babe.
   Where I'm bound, I can't tell.
   Goodbye's too good a word, babe,
   So I'll just say fare thee well.
   I ain't sayin' you treated me unkind.
   You coulda done better, but I don't mind.
   You just kinda wasted my precious time,
   But don't think twice, it's all right.

Hallelujah

Words and Music by Leonard Cohen

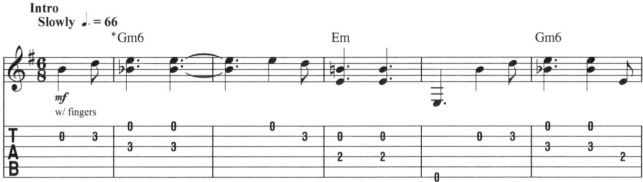

*Optional: To match recording, place capo at 5th fret.

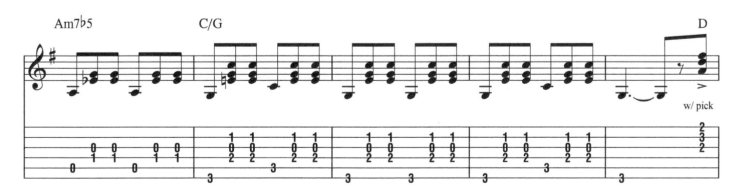

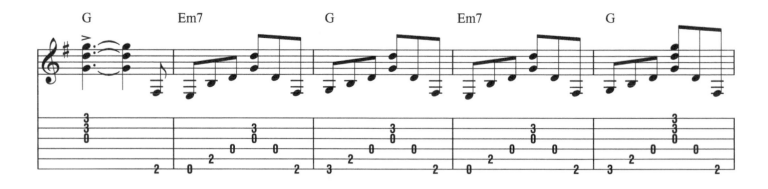

1. Well, I   heard   there __ was   a
2., 3., 4. *See additional lyrics*

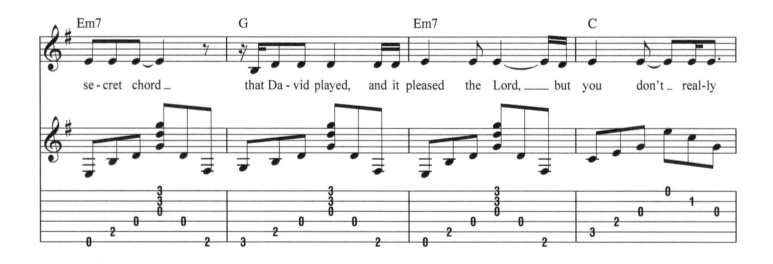

se - cret chord __   that Da - vid played,   and it pleased   the Lord, ___ but you   don't __ real-ly

care   for mu - sic   do __ ya? ___   Well, it   goes   like this,   the

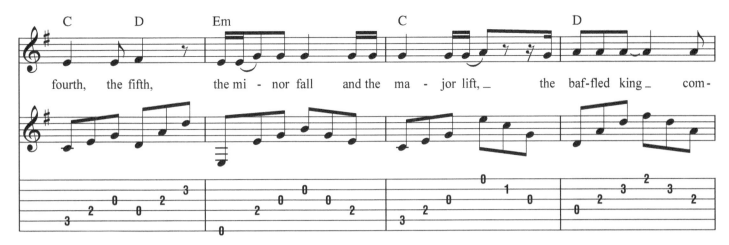

fourth, the fifth, the mi - nor fall and the ma - jor lift, _ the baf-fled king _ com-

Chorus

pos - ing, Hal - le - lu - jah. _____ Hal - le - lu - jah, _____ Hal - le-

lu - jah. _____ Hal - le - lu - jah, Hal - le - lu -

1., 2., 3.
Interlude

- jah. _____ 2. Well,

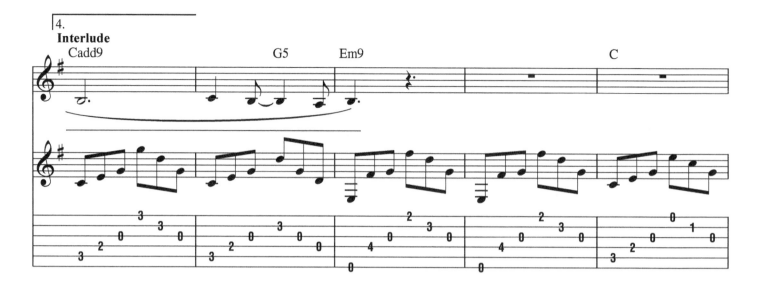

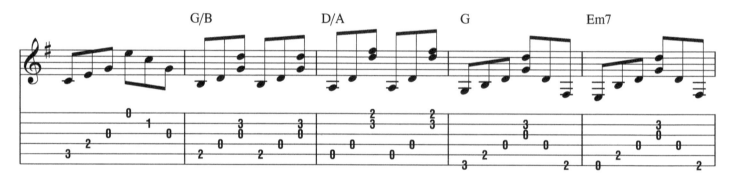

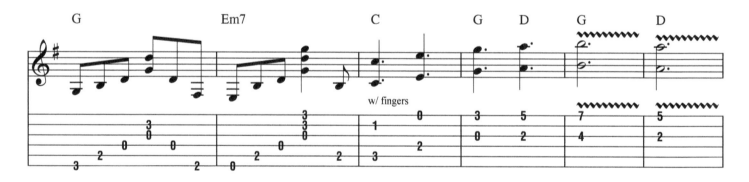

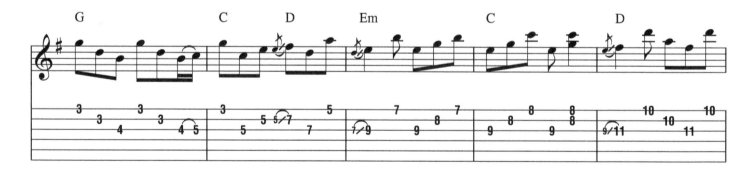

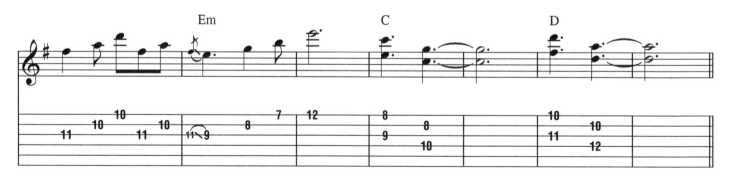

Verse

5. May-be there __ is a God a-bove, __ but all I've __ ev-er learned __ from love __ was

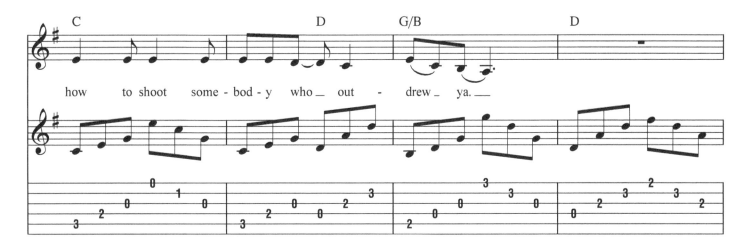

how to shoot some-bod-y who __ out - drew __ ya. __

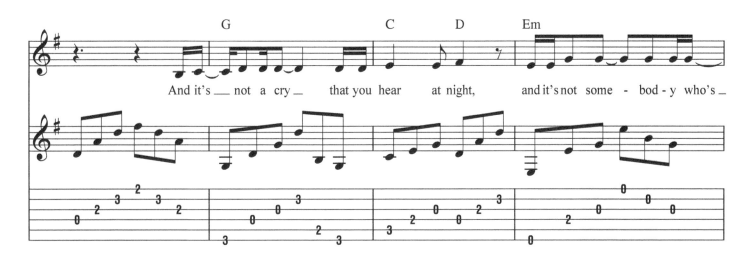

And it's __ not a cry __ that you hear at night, and it's not some - bod - y who's __

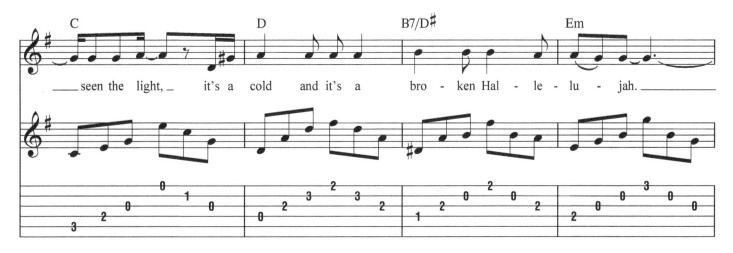

__ seen the light, __ it's a cold and it's a bro - ken Hal - le - lu - jah. _____

39

Chorus

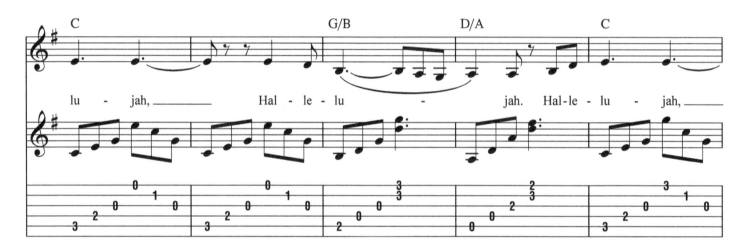

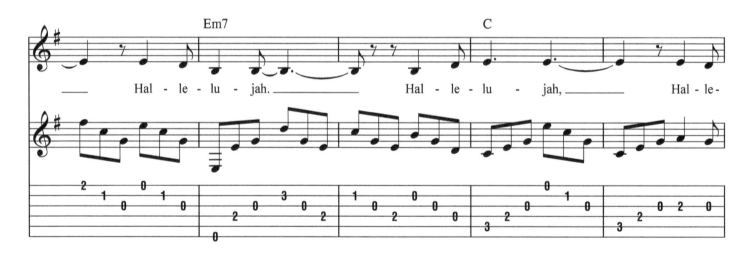

Additional Lyrics

2. Well, your faith was strong but you needed proof.
   You saw her bathing on the roof.
   Her beauty and the moonlight overthrew ya.
   As she tied you to her kitchen chair;
   As she broke your throne and she cut her hair.
   And from your lips you drew the Hallelujah.

3. My baby, I've been here before.
   I've seen this room and I've walked this floor.
   You know, I used to live alone before I knew ya.
   And I've seen your flag on the marble arch,
   And love is not a vict'ry march,
   It's a cold and it's a broken Hallelujah.

4. Well, there was a time when you let me know
   What's really going on below,
   But now you never show that to me, do ya?
   But remember when I moved in you,
   And the Holy Dove was moving too,
   And ev'ry breath we drew was Hallelujah.

Julia

Words and Music by John Lennon and Paul McCartney

Capo II

*Symbols in parentheses represent chord names respective to capoed guitar.
Symbols above reflect actual sounding chords. Capoed fret is "0" in tab.

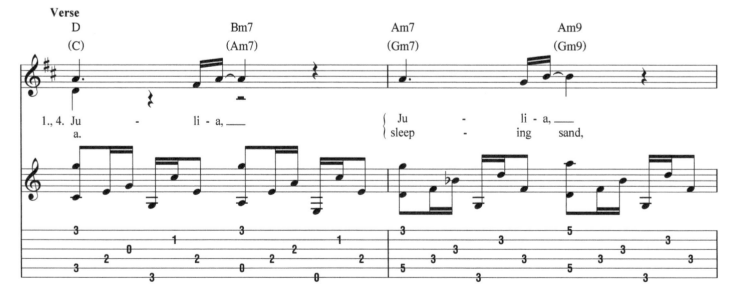

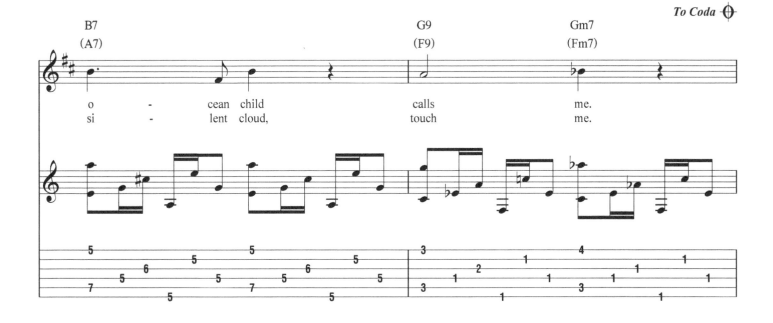

Verse

wind - y smile   calls   me.

So I sing a song _ of love, _ Ju - li - a.

Bridge

Her hair of float - ing sky is shim - mer - ing,

glim - mer - ing   in   the sun.

Verse

3. Ju - li - a, ___ Ju - li - a, ___

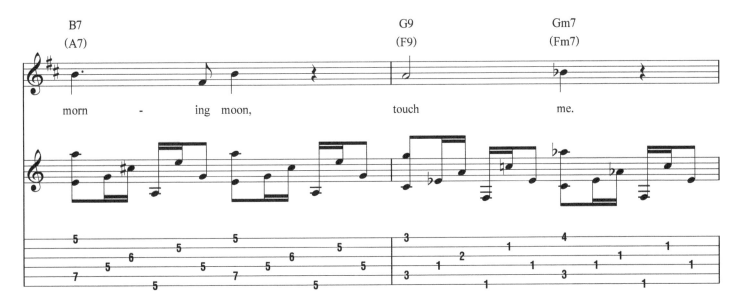

morn - ing moon,   touch   me.

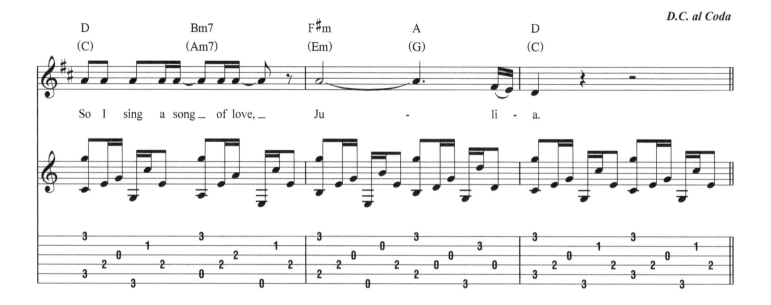

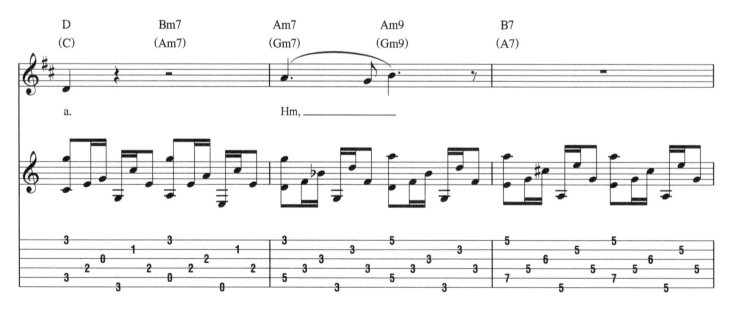

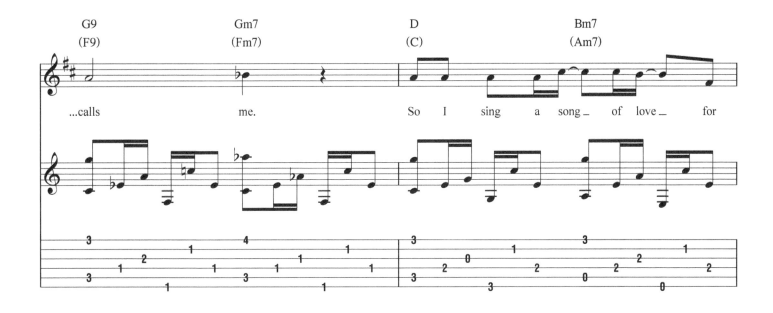

...calls me. So I sing a song of love for

Ju - li - a, Ju - li - a,

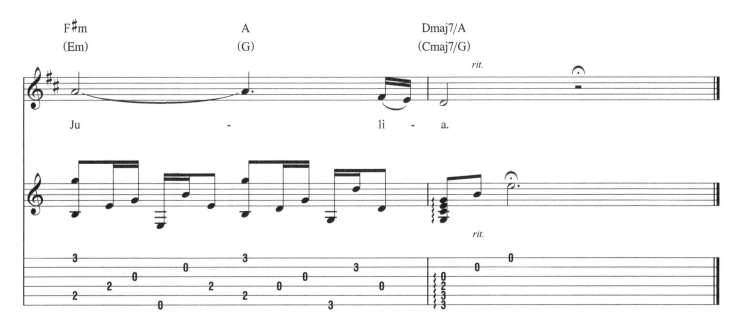

Ju - li - a.

Mister Sandman

Lyric and Music by Pat Ballard

*Refers to downstemmed notes only throughout.

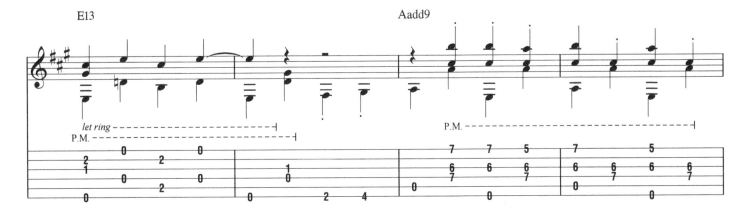

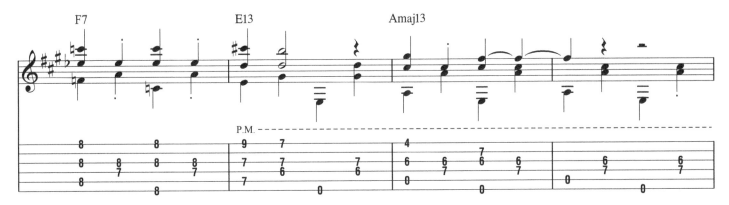

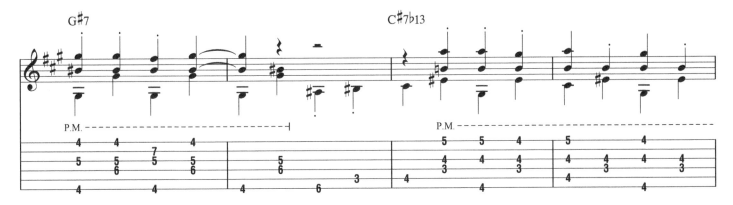

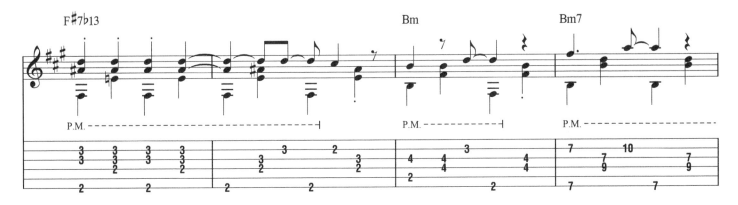

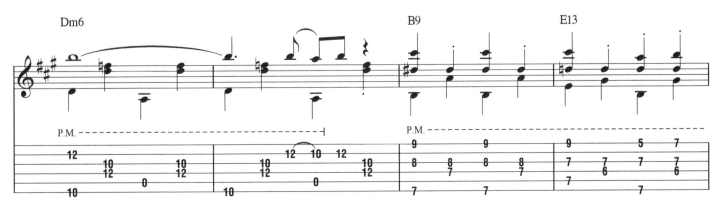

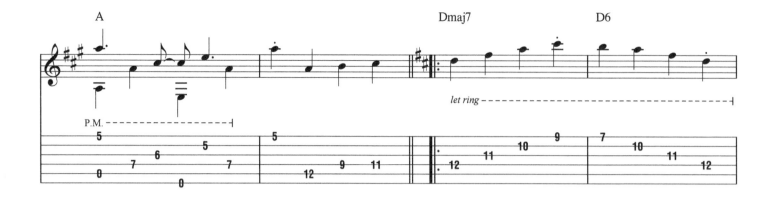

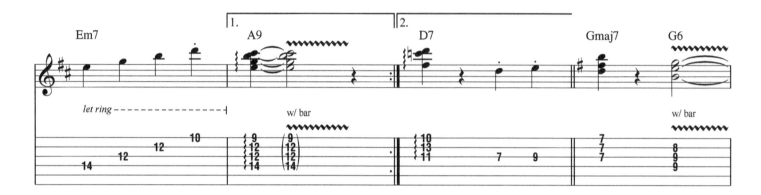

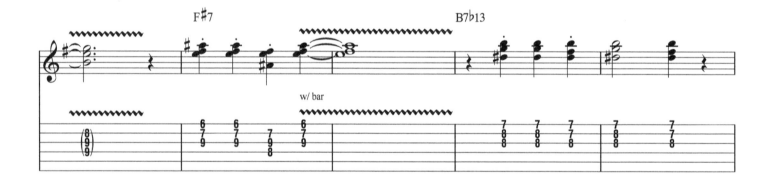

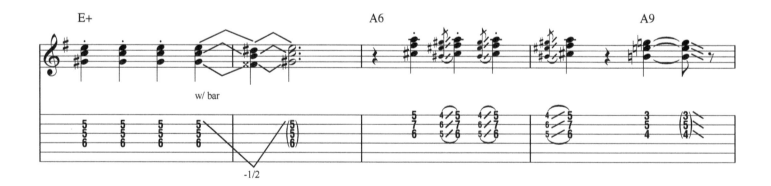

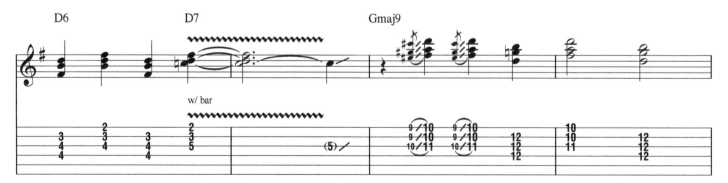

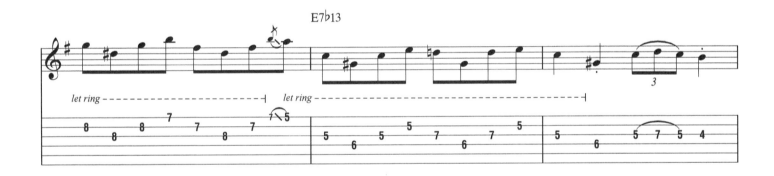

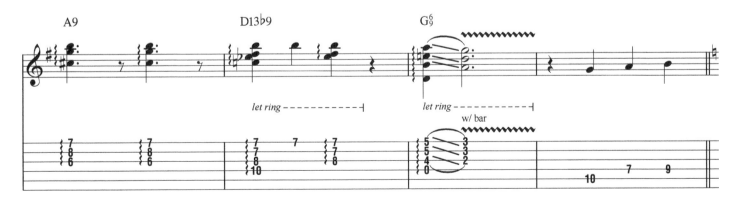

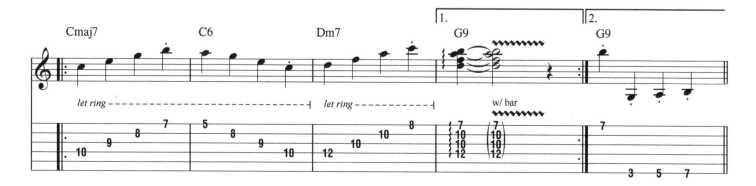

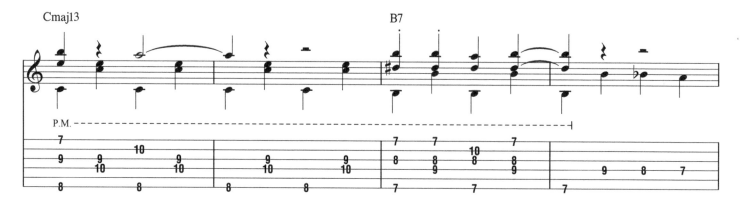

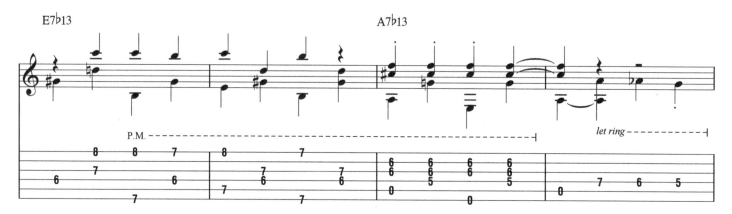

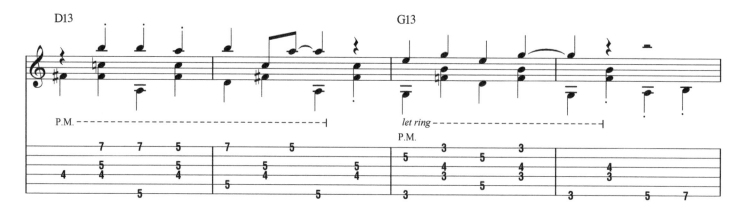

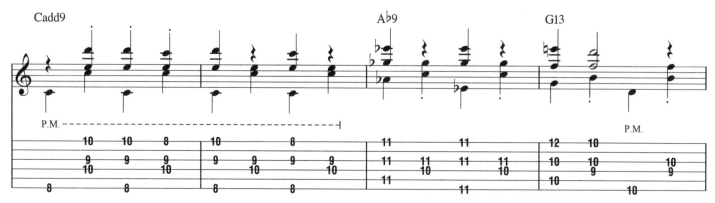

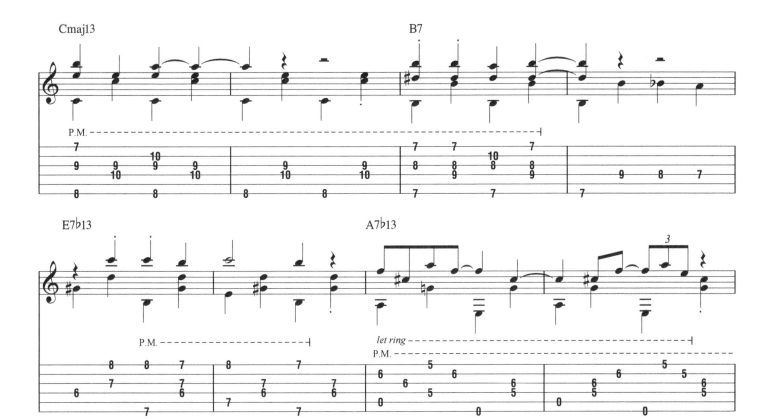

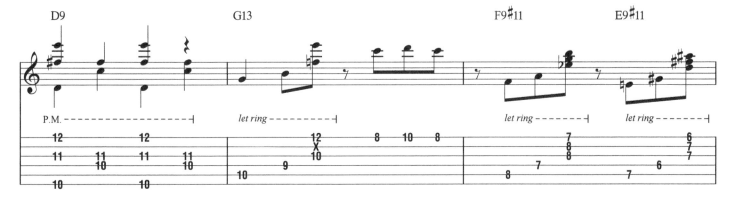

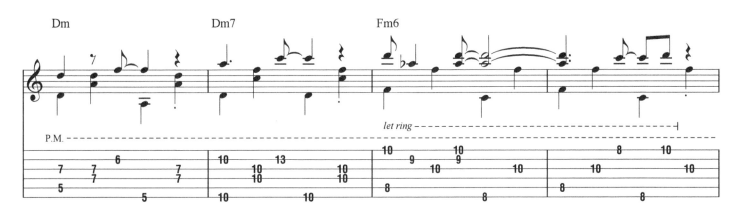

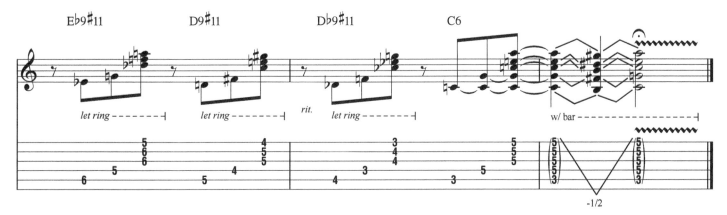

Time in a Bottle

Words and Music by Jim Croce

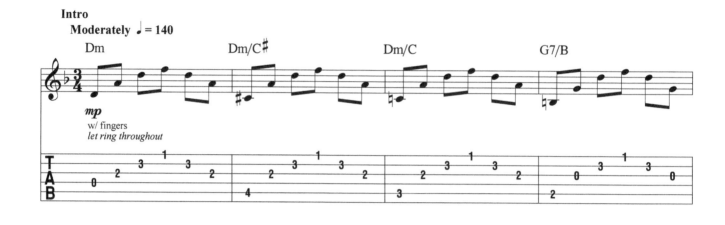

first thing ____ that I'd like to do ____ is to

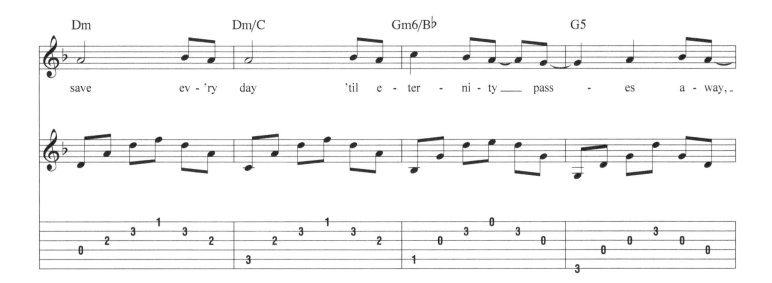

save ev-'ry day 'til e - ter - ni - ty ___ pass - es a - way, _

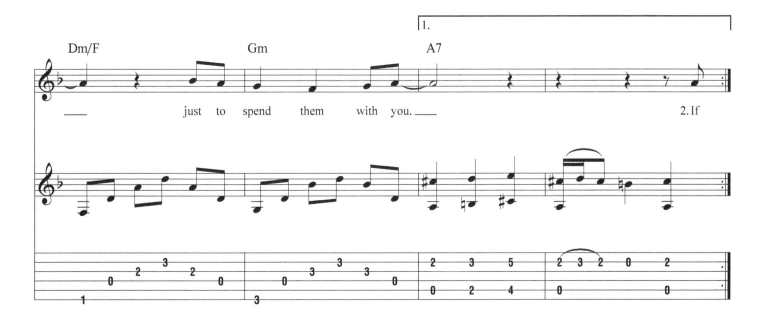

____ just to spend them with you. ___ 2. If

Bridge

But there nev-er seems ____ to be e-nough time ____ to
do the things you want to do once you ____ find them. ____
I've looked a-round e-nough ____ to know ____ that

you're the one   I   want to go through   time   with.

D.C. al Coda
(take 2nd ending)

⊕ **Coda**

Outro

Additional Lyrics

2. If I could make days last forever,
   If words could make wishes come true,
   I'd save ev'ry day like a treasure, and then
   Again I would spend them with you.

3. If I had a box just for wishes,
   And dreams that had never come true,
   The box would be empty except for the mem'ry
   Of how they were answered by you.

You've Got a Friend

Words and Music by Carole King

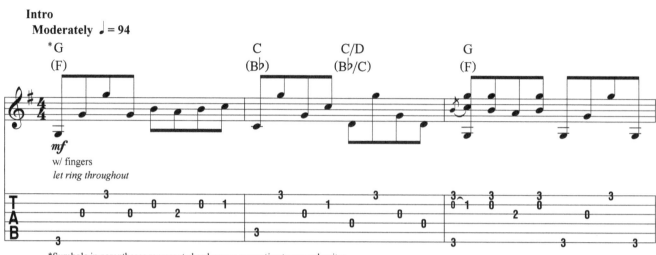

*Symbols in parentheses represent chord names respective to capoed guitar.
Symbols above reflect actual sounding chords. Capoed fret is "0" in tab.

nothing is going right, ___

close your eyes ___ and think of me, and soon I will ___ be there ___

To Coda ⊕

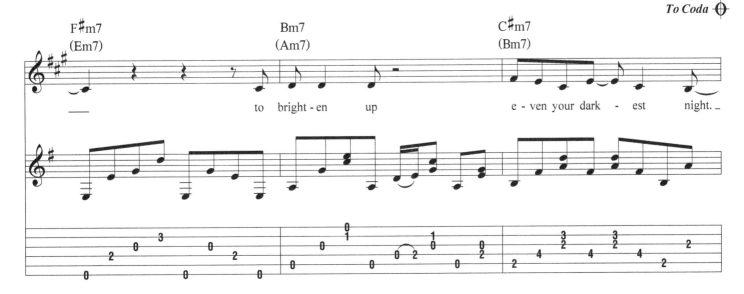

___ to bright-en up even your dark - est night. _

You just call ___ out my ___ name ___

and you know wher-ev-er I am, ___ I'll come run-

- ning, oh ___ yeah, babe, ___ to see you a - gain. ___

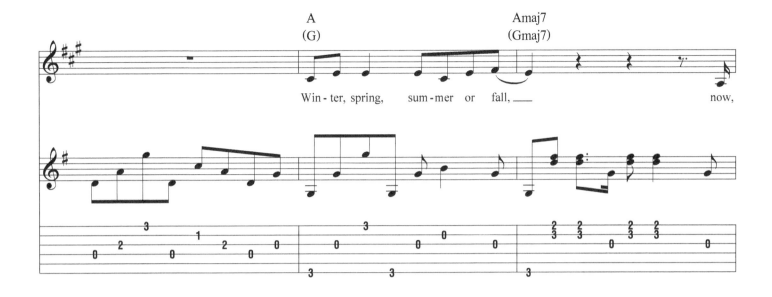

Win - ter, spring, sum - mer or fall, ____ now,

all you got to do _ is __ call, ____ and I'll be there, _____ yeah, _ yeah, yeah. _

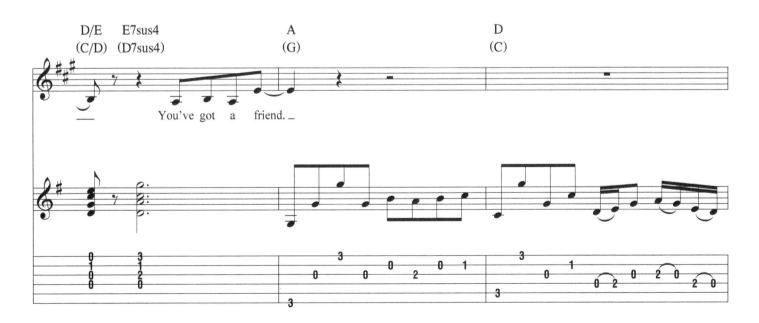

You've got a friend. _

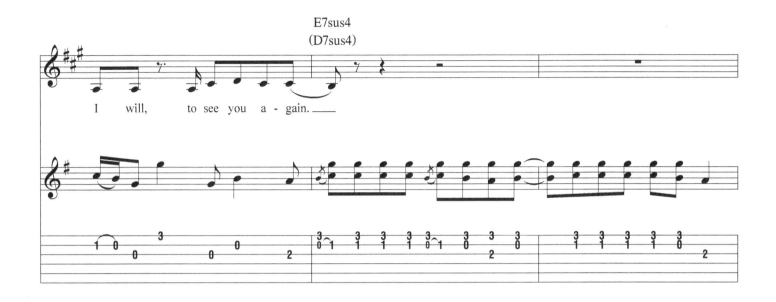

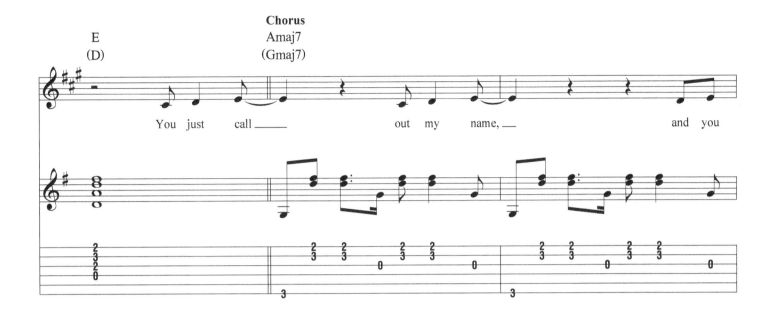

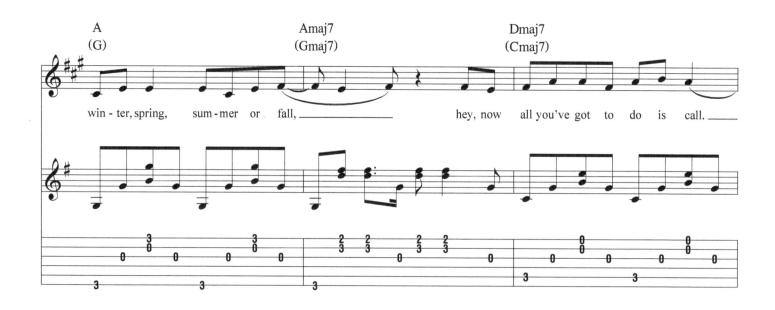

win-ter, spring, sum-mer or fall, _____ hey, now all you've got to do is call. ____

— Lord, I'll be _ there, _ yes I will. ____ You've got a friend. _

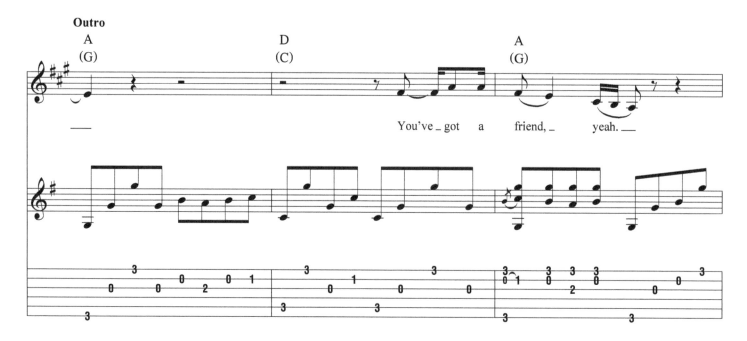

Outro

You've _ got a friend, _ yeah. _

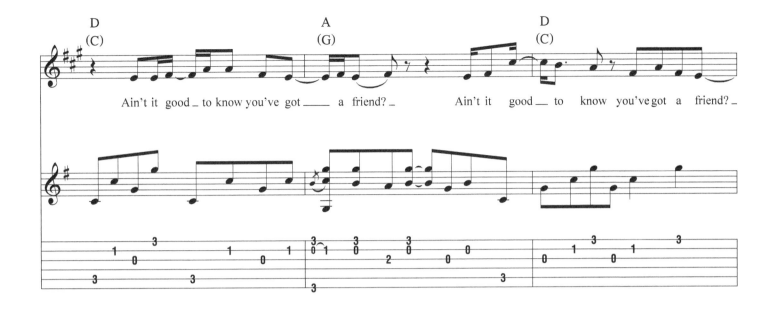

Ain't it good ___ to know you've got ___ a friend? ___ Ain't it good ___ to know you've got a friend? ___

___ Oh, yeah, ___ yeah. ___ You've got a friend. ___

Additional Lyrics

2. If the sky above you grows dark and full of clouds,
   And that ol' North wind begins to blow;
   Keep your head together and call my name out loud.
   Soon you'll hear me knockin' at your door.

Little Martha

Written by Duane Allman

Open E tuning:
(low to high) E-B-E-G#-B-E

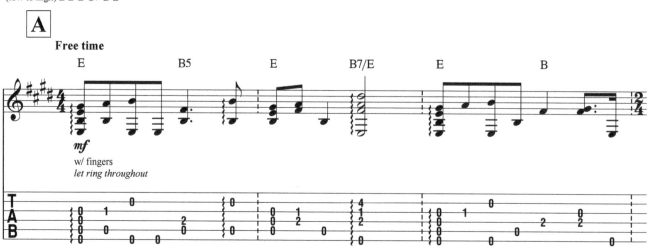

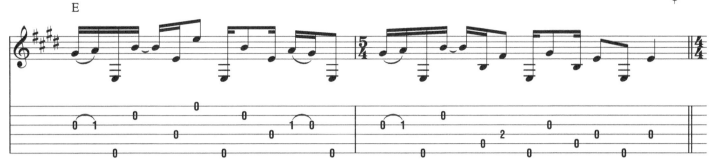

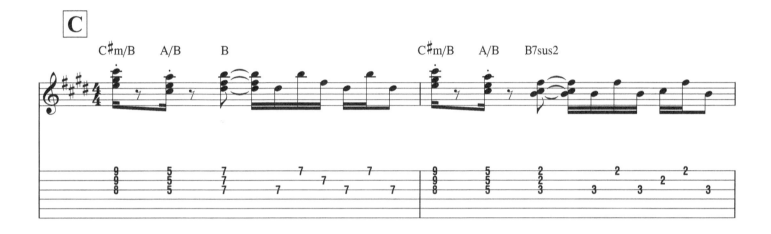

D

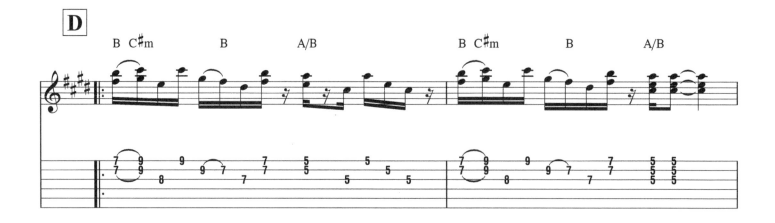

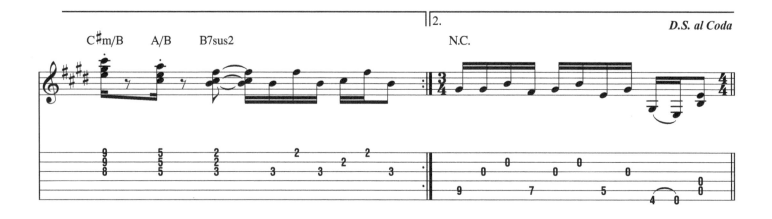

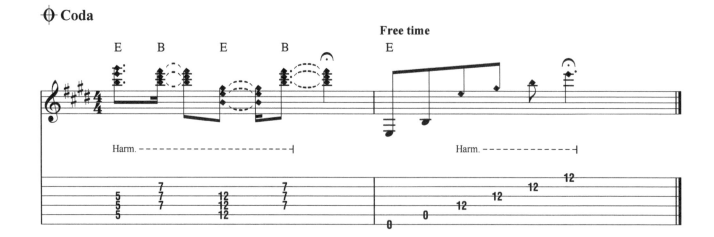

GUITAR NOTATION LEGEND

THE MUSICAL STAFF shows pitches and rhythms and is divided by bar lines into measures. Pitches are named after the first seven letters of the alphabet.

TABLATURE graphically represents the guitar fingerboard. Each horizontal line represents a string, and each number represents a fret.

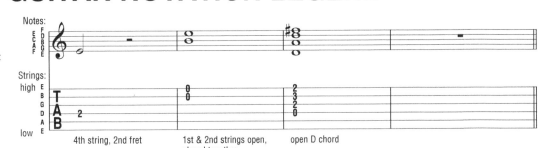

4th string, 2nd fret · 1st & 2nd strings open, played together · open D chord

HALF-STEP BEND: Strike the note and bend up 1/2 step.

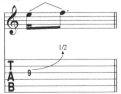

WHOLE-STEP BEND: Strike the note and bend up one step.

GRACE NOTE BEND: Strike the note and immediately bend up as indicated.

SLIGHT (MICROTONE) BEND: Strike the note and bend up 1/4 step.

BEND AND RELEASE: Strike the note and bend up as indicated, then release back to the original note. Only the first note is struck.

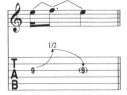

PRE-BEND: Bend the note as indicated, then strike it.

VIBRATO: The string is vibrated by rapidly bending and releasing the note with the fretting hand.

PALM MUTING: The note is partially muted by the pick hand lightly touching the string(s) just before the bridge.

HAMMER-ON: Strike the first (lower) note with one finger, then sound the higher note (on the same string) with another finger by fretting it without picking.

PULL-OFF: Place both fingers on the notes to be sounded. Strike the first note and without picking, pull the finger off to sound the second (lower) note.

LEGATO SLIDE: Strike the first note and then slide the same fret-hand finger up or down to the second note. The second note is not struck.

SHIFT SLIDE: Same as legato slide, except the second note is struck.

TRILL: Very rapidly alternate between the notes indicated by continuously hammering on and pulling off.

TAPPING: Hammer ("tap") the fret indicated with the pick-hand index or middle finger and pull off to the note fretted by the fret hand.

NATURAL HARMONIC: Strike the note while the fret-hand lightly touches the string directly over the fret indicated.

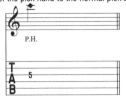

PINCH HARMONIC: The note is fretted normally and a harmonic is produced by adding the edge of the thumb or the tip of the index finger of the pick hand to the normal pick attack.

TREMOLO PICKING: The note is picked as rapidly and continuously as possible.

VIBRATO BAR DIVE AND RETURN: The pitch of the note or chord is dropped a specified number of steps (in rhythm), then returned to the original pitch.

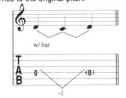

VIBRATO BAR SCOOP: Depress the bar just before striking the note, then quickly release the bar.

VIBRATO BAR DIP: Strike the note and then immediately drop a specified number of steps, then release back to the original pitch.

Additional Musical Definitions

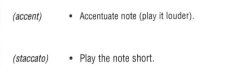

(accent) · Accentuate note (play it louder).

(staccato) · Play the note short.

D.S. al Coda · Go back to the sign (%), then play until the measure marked "*To Coda*," then skip to the section labelled "*Coda*."

D.C. al Fine · Go back to the beginning of the song and play until the measure marked "*Fine*" (end).

Fill · Label used to identify a brief melodic figure which is to be inserted into the arrangement.

N.C. · Harmony is implied.

· Repeat measures between signs.

· When a repeated section has different endings, play the first ending only the first time and the second ending only the second time.

HAL LEONARD GUITAR METHOD

METHOD BOOKS, SONGBOOKS AND REFERENCE BOOKS

THE HAL LEONARD GUITAR METHOD is designed for anyone just learning to play acoustic or electric guitar. It is based on years of teaching guitar students of all ages, and it also reflects some of the best guitar teaching ideas from around the world. This comprehensive method includes: A learning sequence carefully paced with clear instructions; popular songs which increase the incentive to learn to play; versatility – can be used as self-instruction or with a teacher; audio accompaniments so that students have fun and sound great while practicing.

BOOK 1
00699010	Book Only	$8.99
00699027	Book/Online Audio	$12.99
00697341	Book/Online Audio + DVD	$24.99
00697318	DVD Only	$19.99
00155480	Deluxe Beginner Edition (Book, CD, DVD, Online Audio/ Video & Chord Poster)	$19.99

COMPLETE (BOOKS 1, 2 & 3)
00699040	Book Only	$16.99
00697342	Book/Online Audio	$24.99

BOOK 2
00699020	Book Only	$8.99
00697313	Book/Online Audio	$12.99

BOOK 3
00699030	Book Only	$8.99
00697316	Book/Online Audio	$12.99

Prices, contents and availability subject to change without notice.

STYLISTIC METHODS

ACOUSTIC GUITAR
00697347	Method Book/Online Audio	$17.99
00237969	Songbook/Online Audio	$16.99

BLUEGRASS GUITAR
00697405	Method Book/Online Audio	$16.99

BLUES GUITAR
00697326	Method Book/Online Audio (9" x 12")	$16.99
00697344	Method Book/Online Audio (6" x 9")	$15.99
00697385	Songbook/Online Audio (9" x 12")	$14.99
00248636	Kids Method Book/Online Audio	$12.99

BRAZILIAN GUITAR
00697415	Method Book/Online Audio	$17.99

CHRISTIAN GUITAR
00695947	Method Book/Online Audio	$16.99
00697408	Songbook/CD Pack	$14.99

CLASSICAL GUITAR
00697376	Method Book/Online Audio	$15.99

COUNTRY GUITAR
00697337	Method Book/Online Audio	$22.99
00697400	Songbook/Online Audio	$19.99

FINGERSTYLE GUITAR
00697378	Method Book/Online Audio	$21.99
00697432	Songbook/Online Audio	$16.99

FLAMENCO GUITAR
00697363	Method Book/Online Audio	$15.99

FOLK GUITAR
00697414	Method Book/Online Audio	$16.99

JAZZ GUITAR
00695359	Book/Online Audio	$22.99
00697386	Songbook/Online Audio	$15.99

JAZZ-ROCK FUSION
00697387	Book/Online Audio	$24.99

R&B GUITAR
00697356	Book/Online Audio	$19.99
00697433	Songbook/CD Pack	$14.99

ROCK GUITAR
00697319	Book/Online Audio	$16.99
00697383	Songbook/Online Audio	$16.99

ROCKABILLY GUITAR
00697407	Book/Online Audio	$16.99

OTHER METHOD BOOKS

BARITONE GUITAR METHOD
00242055	Book/Online Audio	$12.99

GUITAR FOR KIDS
00865003	Method Book 1/Online Audio	$12.99
00697402	Songbook/Online Audio	$9.99
00128437	Method Book 2/Online Audio	$12.99

MUSIC THEORY FOR GUITARISTS
00695790	Book/Online Audio	$19.99

TENOR GUITAR METHOD
00148330	Book/Online Audio	$12.99

12-STRING GUITAR METHOD
00249528	Book/Online Audio	$19.99

METHOD SUPPLEMENTS

ARPEGGIO FINDER
00697352	6" x 9" Edition	$6.99
00697351	9" x 12" Edition	$9.99

BARRE CHORDS
00697406	Book/Online Audio	$14.99

CHORD, SCALE & ARPEGGIO FINDER
00697410	Book Only	$19.99

GUITAR TECHNIQUES
00697389	Book/Online Audio	$16.99

INCREDIBLE CHORD FINDER
00697200	6" x 9" Edition	$7.99
00697208	9" x 12" Edition	$7.99

INCREDIBLE SCALE FINDER
00695568	6" x 9" Edition	$9.99
00695490	9" x 12" Edition	$9.99

LEAD LICKS
00697345	Book/Online Audio	$10.99

RHYTHM RIFFS
00697346	Book/Online Audio	$14.99

SONGBOOKS

CLASSICAL GUITAR PIECES
00697388	Book/Online Audio	$9.99

EASY POP MELODIES
00697281	Book Only	$7.99
00697440	Book/Online Audio	$14.99

(MORE) EASY POP MELODIES
00697280	Book Only	$6.99
00697269	Book/Online Audio	$14.99

(EVEN MORE) EASY POP MELODIES
00699154	Book Only	$6.99
00697439	Book/Online Audio	$14.99

EASY POP RHYTHMS
00697336	Book Only	$7.99
00697441	Book/Online Audio	$14.99

(MORE) EASY POP RHYTHMS
00697338	Book Only	$7.99
00697322	Book/Online Audio	$14.99

(EVEN MORE) EASY POP RHYTHMS
00697340	Book Only	$7.99
00697323	Book/Online Audio	$14.99

EASY POP CHRISTMAS MELODIES
00697417	Book Only	$9.99
00697416	Book/Online Audio	$14.99

EASY POP CHRISTMAS RHYTHMS
00278177	Book Only	$6.99
00278175	Book/Online Audio	$14.99

EASY SOLO GUITAR PIECES
00110407	Book Only	$9.99

REFERENCE

GUITAR PRACTICE PLANNER
00697401	Book Only	$5.99

GUITAR SETUP & MAINTENANCE
00697427	6" x 9" Edition	$14.99
00697421	9" x 12" Edition	$12.99

For more info, songlists, or to purchase these and more books from your favorite music retailer, go to

halleonard.com

HAL•LEONARD®